$10.95

Feminist Interpretation
of the Bible

PUBLISHED BY THE WESTMINSTER PRESS

Books by Letty M. Russell

Becoming Human (Library of Living Faith)
Growth in Partnership
The Future of Partnership
Human Liberation in a Feminist Perspective—A Theology
Christian Education in Mission

Books Edited by Letty M. Russell

Feminist Interpretation of the Bible

The Liberating Word:
A Guide to Nonsexist Interpretation of the Bible

Feminist Interpretation of the Bible

Letty M. Russell, Editor

The Westminster Press
Philadelphia

ACKNOWLEDGMENTS

Darton, Longman & Todd Ltd and Doubleday & Company, Inc., for verses
from *The Jerusalem Bible* copyright © 1966 by Darton, Longman & Todd
Ltd. and Doubleday & Company, Inc.

International Bible Society, for Scripture quotations marked (NIV) from the
Holy Bible, New International Version. Copyright © 1973, 1978, International
Bible Society.

National Council of the Churches of Christ in the U.S.A., for Scripture
quotations from the Revised Standard Version of the Bible, copyrighted
1946, 1952, © 1971, 1973 by the Division of Christian Education of the
National Council of the Churches of Christ in the U.S.A.

Book design by Gene Harris

First edition

Published by The Westminster Press®
Philadelphia, Pennsylvania

PRINTED IN THE UNITED STATES OF AMERICA

2   4   6   8   9   7   5   3   1

Library of Congress Cataloging in Publication Data
Main entry under title:
Feminist interpretation of the Bible.
  Bibliography: p.
  1. Bible and feminism—Addresses, essays, lectures.
I. Russell, Letty M.
BS680.W7F46 1985   220.6′088042   84-17342
ISBN 0-664-24639-7 (pbk.)

Contents

Contributors

KATIE GENEVA CANNON is Assistant Professor of Christian Ethics at Episcopal Divinity School, Cambridge, Massachusetts. She is the first Afro-American woman to earn her Ph.D. from Union Theological Seminary, New York City (1983), and the first Afro-American woman to be ordained to the ministry by The United Presbyterian Church U.S.A. (1974). Before her studies at Union Seminary she earned an M.Div. degree from Johnson C. Smith University and a B.S. from Barber-Scotia College. She served as a pastor of the Presbyterian Church of the Ascension in New York City (1975–77), as a member of the Administrative Faculty at New York Theological Seminary (1977–80), and as a Research Associate and Visiting Lecturer in Christian Ethics at Harvard Divinity School (1983–84).

J. CHERYL EXUM is Associate Professor of Biblical Studies at Boston College and has both lectured and taught courses and workshops on women in the Bible. She holds a Ph.D. in Hebrew Bible from Columbia University. She is an associate editor of *Semeia: An Experimental Journal for Biblical Criticism* and of the *Catholic Biblical Quarterly* and is a member of the Revised Standard Version Bible translation committee. Her sabbatical year 1983–84 was spent in Jerusalem, conducting research on literary approaches to the Bible, a project she continued the following year in the Federal Republic of Germany as a Fellow of the Alexander von Humboldt Foundation.

MARGARET A. FARLEY is Professor of Christian Ethics at Yale Divinity School. She holds a master's degree in philosophy from the

University of Detroit and a doctorate in religious studies (with specialization in ethics) from Yale University. She has published articles on sexual ethics, medical ethics, feminist theology and ethics, and social ethics in such journals as *Theological Studies, The Journal of Religious Ethics,* and *The Journal of Religion.* She is coauthor of *A Metaphysics of Being and God.*

ELISABETH SCHÜSSLER FIORENZA is Professor of New Testament Studies and Theology at the University of Notre Dame and the author of, among other books, *In Memory of Her: A Feminist Theological Reconstruction of Christian Origins.* She is the author of books on ministries of women in the church and priesthood in the New Testament and of numerous articles on exegetical and theological issues and on feminist theology. She is active in several groups working on the problems of women in church and theology.

SHARON H. RINGE is Associate Professor of New Testament at the Methodist Theological School in Ohio. She earned her doctorate in New Testament at Union Theological Seminary in New York City. She is an ordained minister in the United Church of Christ and a member of the National Council of Churches' Inclusive Language Lectionary Committee and Commission on Faith and Order. She is author of several articles in the fields of New Testament and feminist interpretation.

ROSEMARY RADFORD RUETHER is Georgia Harkness Professor of Applied Theology at Garrett-Evangelical Theological Seminary and Northwestern University in Evanston, Illinois. She received her Ph.D. from Claremont Graduate School, California, and taught at the Howard University School of Religion before going to Garrett. She was also Visiting Lecturer at Yale Divinity School and Harvard Divinity School. She is the author or editor of seventeen books, the most recent of which is *Sexism and God Talk: Toward a Feminist Theology.*

LETTY M. RUSSELL is Professor of the Practice of Theology at Yale Divinity School. She was ordained to the ministry in 1958 by The United Presbyterian Church U.S.A., and served as pastor and educator in the East Harlem Protestant Parish for seventeen years. Her books include *The Future of Partnership, Growth in Partnership,* and *Becoming Human.* She is active in the Commission on Faith and Order of the National Council of Churches and in the World Council of Churches.

KATHARINE DOOB SAKENFELD is Associate Professor of Old Testament at Princeton Theological Seminary, New Jersey. A Presbyterian minister, she has served on the Women's Task Force of the Consultation on Church Union and is a member of the National Council of Churches' Commission on Faith and Order and of the Revised Standard Version Bible Committee. She has published essays on feminist issues and problems in the Hebrew scriptures. Her most recent book is *Faithfulness in Action: Loyalty in Biblical Perspective* (Fortress Press, 1985).

T. DRORAH SETEL is a Jewish educator who studied in the rabbinic program at Leo Baeck College, London, and received her M.T.S. in Hebrew Bible from Harvard Divinity School. She writes, lectures, and teaches on a wide range of topics related to Judaism and feminism and is currently Principal of the Temple Beth Zion Religious School in Buffalo, New York.

SUSAN BROOKS THISTLETHWAITE is Assistant Professor of Theology and Culture at Chicago Theological Seminary. She is an ordained minister in the United Church of Christ and holds a doctorate from Duke University. She is a member of the Inclusive Language Lectionary Committee of the National Council of Churches and was one of the editors of *The Inclusive Language Lectionary, Year A.* Her most recent publications include *Metaphors for the Contemporary Church* and articles in *The Review of Books and Religion, EKU-UCC Working Group Newsletter,* and *Christianity and Crisis.*

PHYLLIS TRIBLE is Baldwin Professor of Sacred Literature at Union Theological Seminary in New York City. She is the author of *God and the Rhetoric of Sexuality* and *Texts of Terror: Literary-Feminist Readings of Biblical Narratives.*

BARBARA BROWN ZIKMUND is Associate Professor of Church History and Academic Dean at Pacific School of Religion, Berkeley, California. She is an ordained minister in the United Church of Christ. A major portion of her teaching and research interests relate to the history of women in American church life. Her most recent book, *Hidden Histories in the United Church of Christ,* deals with the history of women and minorities in that denomination.

Introduction:
Liberating the Word

Letty M. Russell

In 1976 *The Liberating Word: A Guide to Nonsexist Interpretation of the Bible* was published by a small NCCC Task Force on Sexism in the Bible. In the introduction to that book I wrote that the message of the Bible can become a liberating word for those who hear and act in faith but that this same message also needs to be liberated from sexist interpretations which continue to dominate our thoughts and actions. This small book was a "premature" guide to feminist interpretation of the Bible.[1] As the contributions to feminist interpretation have continued to grow in volume and maturity, it has become abundantly clear that the scriptures need liberation, not only from existing interpretations but also from the patriarchal bias of the texts themselves. The more we learn about feminist interpretation, the more we find ourselves asking, with Katharine Sakenfeld, "How can feminists use the Bible, if at all? What approach to the Bible is appropriate for feminists who locate themselves within the Christian community? How does the Bible serve as a resource for Christian feminists?" [55].[2]

This collection of essays does not pretend to have the answer. Rather, it continues the tradition of the earlier book by inviting a wide readership of women and men to share in discussion of these questions. Discussions of feminist perspectives are not taking place in the academy alone. In all parts of the church, many women and not a few men seek ways of liberating the word to speak the gospel in the midst of the oppressive situations of our time. It is hoped that FEMINIST INTERPRETATION OF THE BIBLE will provide resources for collective discussion in Bible study, teaching, and preaching as well as personal study and meditation. As we join together in our study of the Bible, we may even be surprised by the fresh insights and challenges that arise as we search out the meaning of the texts for our own lives.

Fresh insights are needed as the rising consciousness of women and people in the Third World or in other oppressed circumstances leads them to challenge accepted biblical interpretations that reinforce patriarchal domination. From this perspective the Bible needs to be liberated from its captivity to one-sided white, middle-class, male interpretation. It needs liberation from privatized and spiritualized interpretations that avoid God's concern for justice, human wholeness, and ecological responsibility; it needs liberation from abstract, doctrinal interpretations that remove the biblical narrative from its concrete social and political context in order to change it into timeless truth.

Feminist and liberation theologians and biblical scholars have begun working on this process of liberating the word. Reading the Bible from the perspective of the oppressed, they note the bias in all biblical interpretation and call for clear advocacy of those who are in the greatest need of God's mercy and help: the dominated victims of society. These scholars lift up not only the personal but also the social, political, and economic dimensions of the biblical narratives, as they try to reconstruct the hidden history of the "losers." Thus they seek to keep the prophetic and liberating story of God's concern for the oppressed and for the mending of creation alive among communities of faith and faithfulness.

Feminists find that even here the going is difficult, for the biblical texts were written in the context of patriarchal cultures. It is not even clear that the category of the oppressed is "generic" in the worldview of patriarchy [118]. Thus the issue continues to be whether the biblical message can continue to evoke consent in spite of its patriarchal captivity.

The Liberating Word

Perhaps those who wrote *The Liberating Word* were overly optimistic about the possibility of nonsexist interpretation, but they were certainly not so about the growing concern for feminist interpretation in church and school. In the last ten years, such biblical scholars as Phyllis Trible and Elisabeth Fiorenza have published major volumes of interpretation.[3] All the bibliographical references in a book such as this can hardly do justice to the ever-increasing number of books and articles related to this topic. The urgency felt by the original task force in sharing some early reflections with the wider community of faith has been felt by women and men who consider the Bible authoritative for their faith, as well as by those who wish to challenge the impact of patriarchal tradition on the lives of women.

Feminist biblical interpretation has developed into two interdependent areas of research: *inclusive language* and *inclusive interpretation.* Both areas have one thing in common: They are carried forward by cooperating groups of women and men who see their work not only as a scholarly enterprise but also as a collective effort to bring about change in the thoughts, values, and actions of religious groups in the United States and abroad. The original task force was created because of a concern for the interpretation of the Bible that takes place through translation. The National Council of the Churches of Christ in the U.S.A. holds the copyright for the Revised Standard Version of the Bible and continues to sponsor the committee on revisions. Concern for representation of feminist scholarship on the translation committee has led to the appointment of Phyllis Bird, Cheryl Exum, and Katharine Sakenfeld to the committee currently at work on revisions of the Hebrew scriptures. At the same time, subsequent NCCC task forces have developed *An Inclusive-Language Lectionary* for use in worship and preaching.

Like the publication of the RSV before it, the *Lectionary* has sparked a storm of protest. It has made substitutions for key biblical words and concepts: God the Father [and Mother]; God the SOVEREIGN ONE; Realm of God.[4] These may or may not turn out to be the most imaginative renderings, but the greatest outcry has to do with "changing the canon" and thus weakening its "authority." Detractors seldom notice that *The Living Bible* and *The Good News Bible* are also paraphrases, or that the *Reader's Digest* version is also an alteration by deletion of the RSV. The difference is that inclusive changes have to do with imaging God as transcendent of male sexual characteristics or as inclusive of both male and female characteristics. The *Lectionary* confronts the seemingly divinely sanctioned patriarchal view of the world that is the basis of religious security for many people [64].

This book is the fruit of the second stream, cooperative research relative to the inclusive interpretation of the Bible. It seeks particularly to affirm women so that they are acknowledged as fully human partners with men, sharing in the image of God.

Liberating the Word

A group of feminists in the American Academy of Religion and the Society of Biblical Literature decided to make use of the annual meetings to develop a project of feminist hermeneutics (theories of interpretation), seeking to clarify for themselves and for others the distinctive character of feminist interpretation. The participants in the project represented women and men who were concerned about liberating the word from its patriarchal bondage.

The question of liberation hermeneutics has been on the agenda of the Liberation Theology Working Group of the American Academy of Religion and the Society of Biblical Literature for some time. It was the theme of the papers in 1979 and has been the central research topic since 1981. In 1980 a particular focus on feminist hermeneutics was added after an SBL centennial session on "The Effects of Women's Studies on Biblical Studies," moderated by Phyllis Trible. The recognition of the marginalization of women in the biblical field provided an impetus for cooperation among feminist and liberation scholars in asking one another how they do or do not do biblical interpretation differently from the mainstream of biblical study and interpretation.

The published papers from this 1980 meeting[5] indicate that there is a second marginality experienced by feminist biblical scholars: They are marginal to a great deal of feminist scholarship because they continue to uphold the value of the biblical materials in spite of their patriarchal bias against women. For this reason it was important to work together as biblical scholars and theologians to reflect on a particular area of activity: feminist interpretation of the Bible. There had been considerable activity. Some members of this 1981 session had been at work in this area for more than ten years and welcomed a chance to reflect together on this action. They were asking, "What is it that we are doing as feminists when we interpret the Bible? Is there something distinctive about this interpretation? If so, what is it?"

Perhaps the one area that could be agreed upon from the beginning was that, like the nineteen women suffragists who worked with Elizabeth Cady Stanton from 1895 to 1898 to publish *The Woman's Bible,* these women are searching today for a feminist interpretation of the Bible that is rooted in the feminist critical consciousness that women and men are fully human and fully equal. This consciousness is opposed to teachings and actions that reinforce the social system that oppresses women and other groups in society. In her contribution to the centennial session, Dorothy Bass reminded us that Stanton published *The Woman's Bible* because the keystone of misogynist religion and of women's oppression is the Bible.[6] Then as now, there are those who find the Bible irrelevant or hopelessly sexist and others who find feminist critique ungodly, but many women and men struggle to combine a feminist consciousness and serious consideration of the biblical witness with the story of God's presence in the lives of women and men.

The meeting in Dallas in 1981 was preceded by a number of papers seeking to situate the issues of feminist hermeneutic and to examine the options for dealing with the biblical material. Katharine Sakenfeld summarized the options as: (1) looking to texts about women to counteract famous texts "against" women, (2) rejecting the Bible as not authoritative and/or useful, (3) looking to the Bible generally for a liberation perspective, and (4) looking to texts about women to learn from the intersection of the stories of ancient and modern women living in patriarchal cultures [56].[7]

In order to learn about feminist hermeneutics through reflection on action, two feminist exegetical papers were prepared and discussed at the Dallas meeting. (These papers were later published in revised form in the Fall 1983 issue of *Semeia*, devoted to feminist hermeneutics and the Bible, edited by Mary Ann Tolbert.) Sharon Ringe says that her paper on the transfiguration, "Luke 9:28–36: The Beginning of an Exodus," is an elaboration of Sakenfeld's third option; it looks at a particular pericope from a liberation perspective. Her conclusion is that the exegesis is feminist, not in the way she used techniques of historical and literary criticism but in "the concerns, questions, and sensitivities" she brought to the task.

In contrast, Cheryl Exum's paper, "You Shall Let Every Daughter Live: A Study of Exodus 1:8—2:10," was on a text specifically chosen because the courageous action of women is the beginning of the liberation of Israel from Egypt (fourth option). The actions of the midwives and Pharaoh's daughter become extraordinary as we see the risks they took in opposing patriarchy and hear this old story of liberation in new ways.

What did we learn from reflection on these concrete actions of exegesis by feminist scholars? One thing is that, in the words of Phyllis Trible, "feminist hermeneutics embraces a variety of methodologies and disciplines."[8] A second is that the interpretative bias and understanding is built into the exegesis itself, so that it is impossible to delay the feminist or liberation critical perspective until the exegesis is finished, as a sort of theological afterthought about meaning or relevance.[9] Third, as Fiorenza has pointed out, we must seek feminist hermeneutics not just in ways of dealing with the biblical material but in the criteria for evaluating one's approach to scripture.[10]

The New York meeting in 1982 was based on a series of responses to Fiorenza's own proposals for evaluating one's approach to scripture. We attempted to move beyond feminist critical perspective and options for biblical exegesis to the issue of *criteria for feminist interpretation*. In addition to Fiorenza's chapter (published in *The Challenge of Liberation Theology*) and the circulated responses of the

panel, we also considered Rosemary Ruether's first chapter from
Sexism and God Talk, entitled "Feminist Theology: Methodology,
Sources, and Norms." The criteria were not spelled out in great
detail, but it is possible to identify what Ruether calls the "critical
feminist principle" as it is found in these two papers. For Ruether,
the "critical principle of feminist theology is the affirmation and
promotion of the full humanity of women. Whatever denies, diminishes, or distorts the full humanity of women is, therefore, to be
appraised as not redemptive" [115].[11] Fiorenza maintains that
"only the nonsexist and nonandrocentric traditions of the Bible and
the nonoppressive traditions of biblical interpretation have the theological authority of revelation" [128].[12]

From a feminist liberation perspective, feminist theory of inter-
   Both statements immediately raise the issue of our understanding
of biblical authority and canon, as the panelists were quick to point
out. The whole canon is to be taken seriously, especially because of
the possibility of the Bible's use as a tool for the oppression of
women. But it is not considered to function as the Word of God,
evoking consent or faith, if it contributes to the continuation of
racism, sexism, and classism. In her "Response to the Responders"
in New York, Fiorenza asserted that this was not an issue of authority but rather of the political struggles of women against oppression.[13] She seeks to shift the criteria of biblical criticism from a focus
on what is adequate to the human condition and appropriate to
scriptures to what is adequate to historical-literary methods and
appropriate to the struggle of the oppressed for liberation.[14]

   From a feminist liberation perspective, feminist theory of interpretation begins with a different view of reality, asking what is appropriate in light of "personally and politically reflected experience
of oppression and liberation."[15] Interpretation does not begin with
dogmatic statements about the authority of scripture and canon but
rather—as we did in the hermeneutic project—with feminist perspective and praxis. Nevertheless, as we arrive at a critical feminist
perspective that says the biblical text can only be considered to
function as God's word, compelling our faith, when it is nonsexist,
we ourselves have raised the question of authority [137]. The dogmatic and patriarchal view of authority, as timeless truth handed
down, is being challenged by what Fiorenza calls a "paradigm of
emancipatory praxis."[16]

   Issues that have been raised in areas of experience, biblical authority, and models of interpretation need to be pursued in a continuing search, not for an abstract synthesis but for a theory of
interpretation that is rooted in the concrete particularities of oppression and liberation, such as those expressed by Jewish feminist

writers and writers from Black, Hispanic, and Asian perspectives [30, 111].[17] There is much to learn about paradigms of authority from communities of oppressed people such as the Black community, whose members listened to the Bible not for doctrinal propositions but for "experiences which could inspire, convince and enlighten."[18] What is needed is not the old questions and paradigms of authority but the development of new questions and paradigms of authority, which are functional in the communities of struggle wrestling with the biblical text.

The Liberated Word

In all work on feminist and liberation interpretation, a key question is, What would it mean for the Bible to be a liberated word? Liberation from a patriarchal worldview is never a finished task, for the stories continue to be shaped by that view. How then can we hope for a liberated word? Perhaps a clue here is that *the Word of God is not identical with the biblical texts.* The story of these texts is experienced as God's Word when it is heard in communities of faith and struggle as a witness to God's love for the world. This hearing is a gift of the Holy Spirit, which empowers the words so that they may transform lives. In this process of new hearing, the scriptural and church traditions are constantly in need of critique and new interpretation if they are to be liberated as a witness to new situations, cultural perspectives, and challenges.

Another clue is that *liberation is an ongoing process expressed in the already/not yet dynamic of God's action of New Creation.* The word is already liberated as it witnesses to God's liberating action in the story of Israel and of Jesus Christ. It is always in need of liberation from its own historical limitations as well as from those of the interpreters. One day it will be liberated as God's Word comes to be lived out in a New Creation where God has set all things right.

This liberation process usually includes at least four emphases: (1) Feminist and liberation interpreters struggle critically with the texts, using the best resources available to understand the message in the light of the biblical horizon of promise as well as the contemporary situation. (2) They pay close attention to the contexts out of which the message comes, as well as the contexts in the world where it is to be heard. Interpretation, like translation, is an imaginative reconstruction of meaning. (3) For feminists this meaning comes alive most clearly through the community of struggle which seeks to overcome the domination and dehumanization of half the human race. (4) Interpretation is understood as an act of commitment to the poor and the marginal, to whom the good news is addressed as a way of understanding the hoped-for horizon of God's New Creation.

There is no one answer to any of the questions raised by feminist interpretation of the Bible, but in this book we have tried to share some of the journey of interpretation that is taking place among Christian and Jewish feminists. The first section, Feminist Critical Consciousness, explores the question of how women have come to look at biblical texts in a new perspective by looking at the sources for this new angle of vision. Barbara Brown Zikmund and Katie Cannon help us to see the history of this emerging consciousness in the writings of white women and in the struggles of Black women for survival. This is followed by Margaret Farley's discussion of the nature of critical feminist consciousness.

The second section, Feminists at Work, describes feminist biblical exegesis and interpretation. Katharine Doob Sakenfeld provides an overview of feminist uses of biblical materials. Four different approaches to biblical texts follow, each of which highlights the role of mother, wife, or harlot. Sharon Ringe lifts up a liberation perspective that comes from the story of an "uppity woman"; Cheryl Exum takes a new look at mothers in Israel; Drorah Setel and Susan Brooks Thistlethwaite look at the intersection of the ancient stories with our own story to help us see how biblical material must be reinterpreted as part of the critical struggle against patriarchal domination [55, 56].

In the final section, Feminist Critical Principles, the issue of the uniqueness of feminist interpretation is discussed. Rosemary Radford Ruether spells out the correlation between the critical perspective and process of biblical self-critique and the feminist critical perspective on the patriarchal bias of the scriptures. Elisabeth Schüssler Fiorenza develops a feminist interpretive model of critical evaluation. And Letty M. Russell discusses changing perspectives on biblical authority.

In the Postscript, Phyllis Trible reflects on our liberating journey of feminist interpretation since this particular group began a collective search at our Dallas meeting in 1980. She helps us understand more clearly the way in which we have been seeking to liberate the word and highlights the tasks that lie ahead in our continuing interpretive journey.

Part I

Feminist
Critical Consciousness

I

Feminist Consciousness in Historical Perspective

Barbara Brown Zikmund

Why do people change? Sometimes they are forced to change by those who are more powerful. Sometimes they change without even realizing it, growing or evolving along with other developments. Sometimes they feel injustice or limitation and resolve to overcome these difficulties. And sometimes they consciously claim new opportunities never before imagined.

In the last several centuries the situation of women has altered dramatically, especially the circumstances of white women in Western society—so much so that it is possible to document a rising feminist critical consciousness. As women have become more self-conscious about themselves, their relationship to authority, especially religious authority, has changed. Today, Christian and Jewish women have new understandings of their place in religious communities and their relationship to scripture. This new understanding may be called a "feminist critical consciousness."

If we seek to understand what is going on in biblical scholarship today, if we want to celebrate the varieties of women's gifts in church and synagogue, if we want to anticipate some of the work of feminist theologians, it is important to understand the modern history of feminist consciousness. What are its origins? How has it evolved? What are its most recent expressions?

Concern for Woman's Role

Until the early nineteenth century, most intellectual and theological work was done out of a prefeminist perspective. There was no conscious awareness that women's experience, *as* women's experience, was relevant to intellectual work. It was a man's world.

Women were part of the male story. As women they remained invisible. This prefeminist consciousness acknowledged that women's lives did have some unique aspects, but the differences were unimportant.

Gradually, however, women came to believe that their experience was too limited and undervalued. They began to agitate for change: in the legal system, in politics, in fashion, in social expectations, and even in the church. Women became self-conscious about themselves as women.

This was very upsetting to many people. Opponents of the women's rights movement used the Bible to argue that it was not legitimate for women to name or value their female experience. Women in the churches tried to reconcile their commitment to the authority of the Bible with emerging feminist activism. They also became interested in questions of biblical interpretation. How did the Bible affirm their lives? When a text was insensitive to women's experience, what was its authority?

Today many biblical scholars believe that the specific context of interpretation matters. It is important to uncover the ancient circumstances that produced a text. It is also necessary to value the ways in which people of color, the poor, the aging, and women approach the Bible. These unique contexts enhance understanding and shape interpretation. In current biblical study it is almost as important to examine the contemporary situation of the reader as it is to know the particular milieu that produced a text many centuries earlier.

A feminist consciousness in American society, therefore, has gone through several stages.

First, in the face of the new activities and claims of women in the early nineteenth century, many people used the Bible to protect the status quo. They engaged in meticulous literal interpretations of texts to define all differences between men and women. Sometimes these differences uplifted women's status; most of the time they did not. Usually the fact that woman was created second, out of Adam, was treated as evidence that she was inferior to man. In the minds of many, she was not simply different from him, she was subordinate, even evil.

Such negative understandings have a long history. There is an ancient Jewish prayer in which men thank God that they are not women. In the history of doctrine, women were commonly blamed for succumbing to temptation and leading the race into original sin. Many taboos and rituals surrounding women reinforced the understanding that women were unclean and less than men. Some New

Testament texts confirm women as secondary. "But I want you to understand that the head of every man is Christ, the head of a woman is her husband, and the head of Christ is God. . . . For man was not made from woman, but woman from man. Neither was man created for woman, but woman for man" (1 Cor. 11:3, 8); or, "The women should keep silence in the churches. For they are not permitted to speak, but should be subordinate, as even the law says" (1 Cor. 14:34); or, "Let a woman learn in silence with all submissiveness. I permit no woman to teach or to have authority over men; she is to keep silent. For Adam was formed first, then Eve; and Adam was not deceived, but the woman was deceived and became a transgressor" (1 Tim. 2:11–14). Woman is simply less than man.

Sometimes a hierarchical interpretation of woman's fallen or secondary place in creation and redemption was defined positively. Women were different. Out of weakness and sinfulness women showed forth the amazing power of God's grace. If God could save women, God would surely save men. In her secondary status, woman played a special role in God's creation.

By the 1830s and 1840s, many women in America saw the need for different understandings of biblical material. Sarah Grimke, noted antislavery lecturer and women's rights author, charged that the masculine bias of biblical interpretation was part of a deliberate plot against women. In 1837 she called for new feminist scholarship. A few years later, Antoinette Brown, one of the first women to study theology at Oberlin College, examined Paul's epistles with feminist questions. At her ordination in 1853 (she was the first ordained woman in Congregationalism), the preacher, the Rev. Luther Lee, noted that Paul promised new gifts of the Spirit to men and women alike. He discounted some of Paul's specific admonitions against women and quoted from Galatians. "There is neither Jew nor Greek, there is neither slave nor free, there is neither male nor female; for you are all one in Christ Jesus" (Gal. 3:28). A rising feminist consciousness called for discrimination between those parts of the Bible that were essential and those that were culturally relative.

In the 1880s, women under the leadership of Elizabeth Cady Stanton recognized that something needed to be done to counteract the oppressive power of the Bible. A committee of twenty women examined every major passage in the Bible that referred to women and wrote commentaries to expand the interpretive framework. Although the resulting *Woman's Bible* did not use the newest techniques of higher criticism, it presupposed that the Bible ought to be treated like other books, limited by its historical context. Many readers wanted to discover the biblical message without getting bogged down in secondary cultural biases that distorted the freedom of Christian women.

The project was especially noteworthy because it took the Bible seriously. In her introduction to *The Woman's Bible,* Stanton noted that "there are some who write us that our work is a useless expenditure of force over a book that has lost its hold on the human mind." Yet, she continued, "So long as tens of thousands of Bibles are printed every year, . . . it is vain to belittle its influence."[1] More and more women craved freedom from the oppression of the biblical word.

Yet the male scholarly establishment continued to control biblical studies. In 1894 the Society of Biblical Literature voted to admit its first female member. According to Dorothy Bass, who documents the history of women and biblical studies, there was little opposition to the few women members.[2] Most were professors at women's colleges. They were not perceived as a threat. In the early twentieth century, women biblical scholars exhibited strong scholarship but it was never self-consciously feminist. Not until the 1970s did female members of the Society of Biblical Literature (SBL) assert that an intentional feminist hermeneutic was useful in their work.

During much of the nineteenth century, most women compensated for the inequality and marginality they found in society and biblical interpretation by glorifying women's place. If women were created second and limited to special spheres, this was their strength. Women were separate for a reason. God gave women a special calling. Catherine Beecher argued in 1837 that "heaven has appointed to one sex the superior, and to the other the subordinate station, [but] it is not because it was designed that [woman's] duties or her influence should be any the less important." Women in the home had a "sphere of influence" characterized by peace and love. As wives and mothers they served society differently. Men used physical force to gain and keep power, whereas women influenced things in ways that were "altogether different and peculiar."[3] Women brought superior civilizing and Christianizing principles into a world which needed their contribution.

This understanding of women's role was called "soft feminism." It insisted that women were different and that the differences were good. *Vive la différence.* It occurred when women refused to let the negative implications of their supposedly secondary situation dominate their self-image. Knowing about the "other" experience of women gave women special strength.

Out of this attitude, women began to study the lives of great women and to examine the roles of women in the Bible (to capture their unique history and experience). As women came to understand how they were different from men, they learned to capitalize on those differences. In some cases this created a reverse sexism, which declared that the male world could only be saved if it became "feminized."

Concern About Equality

By the early twentieth century, however, women rejected soft feminism and began to promote "women's studies" for egalitarian reasons. They argued that women and men needed to go behind the differences between the sexes to their common humanity. Ultimately, women and men shared one history and condition. Women's experience was important, not because it was special but because women were God's creatures alongside men. Human history was distorted if the experiences of women remained unnoticed and unappreciated. Through women's studies, society could expand areas of knowledge that had been ignored.

At the beginning, the idea of women's studies was not consciously critical, except in its concern for what had been left out. It reached out for the unknown riches of women's contributions, past and present. It sought to capture the totality of woman's history, not necessarily because it was different from male history but because it was a shared history. Justice required that women not remain invisible or secondary.

Initially, women's studies added new courses and programs. Special offerings were created to supplement traditional and classic fields. Women studied these things to discover more about themselves. Historians recovered "herstory." Literary critics examined the works of female writers. Sociologists and psychologists did research on the female life cycle, on violence, on sexuality, and on maternity. Economists and political analysts explored the roles of women as consumers or voters.

Some scholars treated women as one among many minority groups. Women's studies were lumped with Black studies and ethnic studies on the edges of the academic marketplace. Sometimes they were considered a passing fad unrelated to the main corpus of knowledge. As a "minority group," women were not seen to participate fully in the majority culture.

Others argued that women were not a minority. Women were part of every group. Whereas intermarriage blurred the distinctive circumstances of other minority groups, intermarriage by women with the master class (men) was actually the principal source of women's oppression. Women's studies were different from minority studies.

At first women's studies were remedial. They sought to repair damage and correct distortions. They remembered what had been left out. They served the needs of women themselves, by giving a sense of importance and value. They expanded knowledge. Furthermore, because women's studies had no vested interests, their discoveries were freely shared. Women's studies cultivated a new community of persons who celebrated the equal gifts of women and men in history and culture.

In biblical studies, the advent of women's studies expanded women's understandings of biblical authority. By helping everyone appreciate the place of women in the Bible and in the early church, it stretched orthodox assumptions about tradition. It offered alternative images of women. It suggested that more inclusive language could be important for the faith and the church.

Much feminist consciousness-raising is still being done through women's studies. Women need to see the total picture and claim their equality in God's world. Women's groups in church and synagogue appropriately highlight that which has been overlooked. But the journey toward a feminist critical consciousness does not stop with new information or supplemental women's studies. The feminist interpretive task has a critical and creative agenda that goes beyond helping women claim their history and see their place in society. It enables women to praise God in this "strange land," *and* it criticizes the distortions perpetuated by the majority. In its fullness, a feminist critical consciousness strives to develop an authentic inclusive interpretive framework for all biblical, historical, and theological work.

Feminist Consciousness

In the movement from women's studies to feminist studies, two things happened: first, the new material and methods cultivated in women's studies became the basis for a critique of past assumptions and paradigms. Enthusiasm about new knowledge turned into a critique of old knowledge. Second, a feminist critical consciousness, in relationship with other liberation movements, began to shape an entirely new interpretative framework.

Women in the mid-twentieth century came to feel that reinterpretation was not enough. It was essential to deal with patriarchal tradition itself. How should women and men who accepted the promise of liberation deal with the Bible and the church today?

Strictly speaking, women's studies cared only about those aspects of life where women played a part. A feminist consciousness, however, was not limited to women. Inclusive questions needed to be asked about every biblical text and every event in church history: What difference did it make that women were or were not included? If women were not taken into account, why? The answers to these questions challenged many sacred principles of doctrine and practice.

In our times, an emerging feminist consciousness attacks majority positions and points out the injustices of history. Feminists are angry, iconoclastic, and revolutionary. A feminist critical consciousness does not always state positively what it stands for, but it knows and names its enemies. Feminism does not simply stretch the horizons of knowledge, it alters the landscape by tearing down many of the old patriarchal buildings.

Feminism has to be very careful, however, that its criticism is not co-opted by an establishment mind-set. For example, if feminists uncover the importance of women's ministries in the early church and become highly critical of the contemporary church, they cannot turn around and insist that women ought to have access to the accumulated power and privilege enjoyed by male clergy through the ages. Giving power and privilege to women who have been denied it historically does not do away with the problems of patriarchy.

Virginia Woolf wrote about the dilemma women confront when they try to move into arenas previously dominated by men:

> For we have to ask ourselves, here and now, do we wish to join that [academic] procession, or don't we? On what terms shall we join that procession? Above all, where is it leading us, the procession of educated men? . . . Let us never cease from thinking,—what is this "civilization" in which we find ourselves? What are these ceremonies and why should we take part in them? What are these professions and why should we make money out of them? Where in short is it leading us, the procession of the sons of educated men?[4]

The ultimate aim of a feminist consciousness is to make the experience and insights of women available to the entire world, not simply to know more about women in and of themselves. Yet if we are to include women in the total picture, we are called to rethink how we interpret everything. A canon that is inclusive is self-correcting and constantly reinterpreting God's ways with this world. A history that is inclusive involves different periodization, different content, and different emphases. And because our religious faith is grounded in the historical experience of Jews and Christians expressed through scripture and lived out through history, a feminist critical consciousness must build a theology by moving beyond criticism to constructive alternatives.

The feminist critical consciousness in the late twentieth century has been greatly influenced by the development of the so-called "woman's liberation movement." In that context women have explored together the realities of women's oppression, found support for a growing conviction that the personal is political, and celebrated the power of consciousness-raising experiences. Feminists in secular and religious studies build upon this common context to reshape their disciplines.

Contemporary feminists approach reality with new questions and formulate new interpretations. The motive is not simply to reform; it is to reconstruct. A mature feminist critical consciousness is revolutionary. It challenges method and upsets assumptions. Very early in the evolution of feminism, Mary Daly predicted that this would happen, because

> the tyranny of methodolatry hinders new discoveries. It prevents us from raising questions never asked before and from being illumined by ideas that do not fit into pre-established boxes and forms. . . . Under patriarchy, Method has wiped out women's questions so totally that even women have not been able to hear and formulate our own questions to meet our own experiences.[5]

As a critical feminist consciousness comes of age, the situation is further complicated by the fact that religion is different. We do not just study religion, we live it. Changes in religious questions and assumptions affect people deeply. With religion the personal is not just political, it is ontological: that is, it informs our entire way of being and relating to God, not simply our situation in the sociopolitical order.

Against this reality, feminists in religion are developing new methods for liberating their faith from patriarchal patterns. Feminists are seeking alternative interpretive frameworks for biblical, historical, and theological work. Feminists are using different materials to enrich their faith. And in all cases, feminists are trying to do this in an uncompetitive collegial style.

Two patterns of feminist work have emerged in religious studies. The scholars in this book represent those feminists who refuse to give up on the liberating power of the scriptures. They seek new ways to understand the normative authority of the Bible in their faith. Other feminists fear this is impossible. Both groups agree that patriarchy must be overcome, but they differ in their understanding of how.

Jewish and Christian feminists use new interpretive principles to liberate God's word in scripture. They are willing to risk, out of a belief that God has promised liberation to all creation. They are redefining authority to celebrate the resources of community in interpreting God's Word. By allowing women's experience to inform the task, they are discovering new theologies and leaving behind old oppressions.

Feminists who feel that the Bible and its theological/ecclesiastical traditions must be left behind focus upon the sacrality of women and seek to recover the rich religious insights of Goddess traditions. This approach may be called pagan. Yet even for those who want to stay within the Jewish and Christian legacy, the work of neo-pagan or nonbiblical feminist spirituality is important. Goddess religions have powerful symbols that stretch our understanding of religious practice and human experience.

Both groups emphasize that feminist perspectives in faith and practice enrich religion. They name oppression, celebrate the personal, and explore the nature of community. They believe that only when the patriarchal repression of women and women's religious experience is replaced with religious faith and practice affirming a healthy relationship to the holy can the human religious spirit be truly free.

The development of a feminist critical consciousness has moved from the innocent assumption that women's experience was irrelevant to the conviction that it is normative. There were (and are) those who insist that differences between men and women forced women into separate spheres of life and responsibility. Women were viewed as subordinate. Sometimes, women's situation (though separate) was considered equal and even superior. Women's studies took society beyond this double standard and invited women to discover the unknown and unexplored parts of their story. Women's studies presupposed that men and women were equal. Eventually, new knowledge led to a critique of old assumptions, which in turn shaped a new feminist critical consciousness.

Dealing with the Bible through all of this has not been easy. Sometimes it has been common to ignore scripture and avoid questions of authority. Many women of faith, however, are not willing to give up. They believe that the Bible offers a liberating word for our times and that the feminist critical consciousness which has emerged over the last century can unlock new meaning in scripture. Contemporary feminists are asking new questions and forging new theories to enrich the religious understanding of all women and men.

2

The Emergence
of Black Feminist
Consciousness

Katie Geneva Cannon

The feminist consciousness of Afro-American women cannot be understood and explained adequately apart from the historical context in which Black women have found themselves as moral agents. By tracking down the central and formative facts in the Black woman's social world, one can identify the determinant and determining structures of oppression that have shaped the context in which Black women discriminately and critically interpret scripture, in order to apprehend the divine Word from the perspective of their own situation. Throughout the history of the United States, the interrelationship of white supremacy and male superiority has characterized the Black woman's reality as a situation of struggle—a struggle to survive in two contradictory worlds simultaneously, one white, privileged, and oppressive, the other black, exploited, and oppressed. Thus, an untangling of the Black religious heritage sheds light on the feminist consciousness that guides Black women in their ongoing struggle for survival.

The Struggle for Human Dignity

The Black church is the crucible through which the systematic faith affirmations and the principles of biblical interpretation have been revealed. It came into existence as an invisible institution in the slave community during the seventeenth century. Hidden from the eyes of slave masters, Black women, along with Black men, developed an extensive religious life of their own. Utilizing West African religious concepts in a new and totally different context and syncretistically blending them with orthodox colonial Christianity, the slaves made Christianity truly their own. C. Eric Lincoln puts it this way:

> The blacks brought their religion with them. After a time they accepted the white man's religion, but they have not always expressed it in the white man's way. . . . The black religious experience is something more than a black patina on a white happening. It is a unique response to a historical occurrence that can never be replicated for any people in America.[1]

The biblical interpretation of the antebellum Black church served as a double-edged sword. Confidence in the sovereignty of God, in an omnipotent, omnipresent, and omniscient God, helped slaves accommodate to the system of chattel slavery. With justice denied, hopes thwarted, and dreams shattered, Black Christians cited passages from the Bible that gave them emotional poise and balance in the midst of their oppression. In the prayer meetings and song services, in the sermons and spirituals, the biblical texts provided refuge in a hostile white world. Howard Thurman argued that this stance enabled enslaved Black women and Black men to make their worthless lives worth living.[2] "Being socially proscribed, economically impotent, and politically brow-beaten," Benjamin Mays wrote, "they sang, prayed, and shouted their troubles away."[3]

The biblical interpretation of the Black church also made the slaves discontent with their servile condition. Under slavery the Black woman had the status of property: Her master had total power over her, and she and her children were denied the most elementary social bonds—family and kinship. The Black woman was defined as "brood sow" and "work ox." Concession was given to her gender only when it was expedient for the slaveowner. Much of the theology of this period encouraged slave women to eliminate the sources of their oppression. The Black religious experience equipped slaves with a biblical understanding that called them to engage in acts of rebellion for freedom. The faith assertions of the Black church encouraged slaves to reject any teachings that attempted to reconcile slavery with the gospel of Jesus Christ. As George Rawick points out:

> It was out of the religion of the slaves, the religion of the oppressed, the damned of this earth, that came the daily resistance to slavery, the significant slave strikes, and the Underground Railroad, all of which constantly wore away at the ability of the slave masters to establish their own preeminent society.[4]

The slave woman's religious consciousness provided her with irrepressible talent in humanizing her environment. Having only from midnight to daybreak to provide love and affection for her own offspring, the Black woman returned at night with leftovers, throwaways, discarded shells of the white slaveowner's rubbish to the small, crude, squalid dwelling where she made a home for her family. Often she took into her quarters Black children whose parents had been sold away from them or they from their parents with the full knowledge that she could expect to have her own offspring with her for a few years, at the most.

When the state laws adopted the principle of *partus sequitur ventrem* —the child follows the condition of the mother regardless of the race of her mate—the Black woman became the carrier of the hereditary slave status. Absolving all paternal responsibilities, this principle institutionalized and sanctioned sexual prerogatives and the rape of Black women by white men. No objective circumstances such as education, skill, dress, or manner could modify this racist arrangement. The Black woman's slave status extended to her children and her children's children, a lifetime of abject servitude, supposedly to the infinity of time [99].

Being both slave and female, the Black woman survived wanton misuse and abuse. She was answerable with her body to the sexual casualness of "stock breeding" with Black men and to the sexual whims and advances of white men. Virtually all the slave narratives contain accounts of the high incidence of rape and sexual coercion. La Frances Rodgers-Rose, in *The Black Woman,* describes the sexual exploitation of the Black slave woman in this manner:

> The Black woman had to withstand the sexual abuse of the white master, his sons and the overseer. A young woman was not safe. Before reaching maturity, many a Black woman had suffered the sexual advances of the white male. If she refused to succumb to his advances, she was beaten and in some cases tortured to death.[5]

White men, by virtue of their economic position, had unlimited access to Black women's bodies. At the crux of the ideology that Black women were an inferior species was the belief that Black women, unlike white women, craved sex inordinately. "The rape of the black woman by white men or the use of their bodies for pleasure could be rationalized as the natural craving of the black women for sex, rather than the licentiousness of the white men."[6] The mixed blood of thousands upon thousands of African peoples' descendants is incontrovertible proof of sexual contact between white slave masters and Black slave women.

Reduced to subservient marginality, the Black slave woman was constantly being stripped of familiar social ties in order for her owner to maximize his profit. All of the Black woman's relationships existed under the shadowy threat of a permanent separation. As an outsider in society, the Black woman lived with constant fear, and most of the time she had to endure the reality of having her husband and her children sold away from her in the likelihood that she would never see them again. Countless slave families were forcibly disrupted. "This flow of enslaved Afro-Americans must count as one of the greatest *forced* migrations in world history."[7]

> In nothing was slavery so savage and so relentless as in its attempted destruction of the family instincts of the negro [sic] race in America. Individuals, not families; shelters, not homes; herding, not marriages, were the cardinal sins in that system of horrors. Who can ever express in song or story the pathetic history of this race of unfortunate people when freedom came, groping about for their scattered offspring with only instinct to guide them, trying to knit together the broken ties of family kinship?[8]

The Black woman's consciousness in the first two centuries of the American colonies' existence focused on identifying resources that would help her sustain the inescapable theological attacks—either Black people were human beings and could not be property, or they were property and something less than human. "Black and white were constantly presented as antipodes, negative and positive poles on a continuum of goodness. In the minds of whites, Negroes stood as the antithesis of the character and properties of white people."[9] All of life was graded according to an elaborate hierarchy, inherited from the Middle Ages, known as the "great chain of being." Blacks were assigned a fixed place as an inferior species of humanity. The common property of white culture were certain preconceptions about the irredeemable nature of Black women and Black men as "beings of an inferior order,"[10] a species between animal and human. Unwavering faith in God provided Black Christians with patience and perseverance in the ongoing struggle for survival [143].

The Struggle Against White Hypocrisy

The institution of chattel slavery in America was destroyed by the most momentous event of the nineteenth century, the Civil War, from 1861 to 1865. Emancipation removed the legal and political slave status from approximately four million Black people in the United States, which meant that, in principle, these Blacks owned their person and their labor for the first time. Unfortunately, for the vast majority of Afro-Americans, the traditional practices of racial and gender subordination subjected them to incredible suffering after the war. The general patterns of de facto social segregation and disenfranchisement of Blacks, which were integral to the *raison d'être* of the peculiar institution, continued as the norm. White Southerners accepted the abolition of slavery as one of the consequences of their military defeat and surrender at Appomattox in 1865, but they were totally unwilling to grant Black women and men respect as equal human beings with rights of life, liberty, and property. The "rightness of whiteness" counted more than the basic political and civil rights of any Black person. Southern apologists received widespread acceptance from many Northerners who had opposed slavery on the ground of an indivisible United States while avidly supporting racial subordination. Many academic historians, sociologists, anthropologists, theologians, and biblical scholars dredged up every conceivable argument to justify the natural inferiority of Blacks and their natural subordination to whites. Institutional slavery ended, but the virulent and intractable hatred that supported it did not.

During the Reconstruction Era, the Black church continued to assume its responsibility for shaping the expository and critical biblical reflections that would help the adherents of the faith understand the interplay of historical events and societal structures. The biblical teachings of the church continued to develop out of the socioeconomic and political context in which Black people found themselves. In every sphere where Black people were circumscribed and their legal rights denied, the Black church called its members to a commitment of perfecting social change and exacting social righteousness here on earth. The scripture lessons that were most important after emancipation were those texts which focused on Christians working to help the social order come into harmony with the divine plan.

When the Freedmen's Bureau was effectively curtailed and finally dismantled, Blacks were left with dead-letter amendments and nullified rights acts, with collapsing federal laws and increasing white terrorist violence. Beyond the small gains and successes of a few Blacks, the optimism of ex-slaves about full citizenship was soon extinguished. Hence, the aftereffects of Reconstruction and their consequences called the Black church forth as the community's sole institution of power. Whether urban or rural, the Black church was the only institution totally controlled by Black people. It was the only place outside the home where Blacks could express themselves freely and take independent action. The church community was the heart, center, and basic organization of Black life. And those who were the religious leaders searched the scriptures to give distinctive shapes and patterns to the words and ideas that the Black community used to speak about God and God's relationship to an oppressed people.

The Black woman began her life of freedom with no vote, no protection, and no equity of any sort. Black women, young and old, were basically on their own. The patterns of exploitation of the Black woman as laborer and breeder were only shaken by the Civil War; by no means were they destroyed. Throughout the late nineteenth and early twentieth century, Black women were severely restricted to the most unskilled, poorly paid, menial work. Virtually no Black woman held a job beyond that of domestic servant or field hand. Keeping house, farming, and bearing and rearing children continued to dominate all aspects of the Black woman's life. The systematic exclusion and routinized oppression of Black females from other areas of employment served as confirmations for the continuation of the servile status of Black women. As Jeanne Noble describes it, "While freedom brought new opportunities for black men, for most women it augmented old problems."[11] After emancipation, racism and male supremacy continued to intersect patriarchal and capitalist structures in definitive ways.

The religious consciousness of the Black freedwoman focused on "uplifting" the Black community. The Black female was taught that her education was meant not only to uplift her but also to prepare her for a life of service in the overall community. It was biblical faith grounded in the prophetic tradition that helped Black women devise strategies and tactics to make Black people less susceptible to the indignities and proscriptions of an oppressive white social order.

The unique alliance between northern missionary and philanthropic societies afforded an increasing number of Black women opportunities of education. The Black woman as educator attended Sunday services at local churches, where she often spoke in order to cultivate interest in the Black community's overall welfare. Churchwomen were crusaders in the development of various social-service improvement leagues and aid societies. They sponsored fund-raising fairs, concerts, and all forms of social entertainment, in order to correct some of the inequities in the overcrowded and understaffed educational facilities in the Black community. These dedicated women substantially reduced illiteracy among Black people.

The biblical teachings of the Black church served as a bulwark against laws, systems, and structures that rendered Black people as nonentities. Fearful of the emerging competitive race relations with Blacks, white America instituted a whole set of policies and customs in order to maintain white supremacy. White people wanted to regulate and eventually stamp out all notions of social equality between the races. Terror of Black encroachment in areas where whites claimed power and privileges even caused southern state legislatures to enact Black Codes, similar to slave codes, designed to limit drastically the rights of ex-slaves.

> Although their provisions varied among states, the Black Codes essentially prevented the freedmen from voting or holding office, made them ineligible for military service, and disbarred them from serving on juries or testifying in court against whites. Moreover, blacks were forbidden to travel from place to place without passes, were not allowed to assemble without a formal permit from authorities, and could be fined and bound out to labor contractors if they were unwilling to work.[12]

"Jim Crowism" became a calculated invidious policy to exclude the mass of Black folk from interracial contacts in public places and on public transportation facilities. With *de jure* segregation, civil rights for Black people fell outside the realm of legal contract. Not only were Blacks granted no protection under the law, but direct steps were taken to control even the most personal spatial and social aspects of Black life. "It became a punishable offense against the laws or the mores for whites and Negroes to travel, eat, defecate, wait, be buried, make love, play, relax and even speak together, except in the stereotyped context of master and servant interaction."[13] Segregation took a less blatantly visible form in the North, but it was only slightly less rigid.

The Black woman's consciousness during this period caused her to evaluate this extreme social impoverishment—caused by a panoply of state laws requiring a rigid system of segregation—as an abominable evil. She believed that Jim Crowism was contrary to nature and against the will of God. The Black church with its own ideas of morality condemned the hypocrisy of white Christians. How could Christians who were white refuse flatly and openly to treat as fellow human beings Christians who had African ancestry? Was not the essence of the gospel mandate a call to eradicate affliction, despair, and systems of injustice? The Black church's identification with the children of Israel was a significant theme in the consciousness of the Black woman.

During the migratory period (1910–1925), the Black church was the citadel of hope. A series of floods and boll weevil infestations, diminishing returns on impoverished soil, wartime curtailment of European immigrants for industrial labor markets, and rampaging racial brutality accelerated Black emigration from South to North and from rural to urban areas. Tens of thousands of Black women and men left home, seeking social democracy and economic opportunities. Black churches were used for almost every sort of activity: as boarding quarters for migrant people who had nowhere else to go, as centers for civic activities, as concert halls for artists and choirs, and as lecture rooms for public-spirited individuals. During this colossal movement of Black people, the church continued to serve as the focal point for the structure of Black life.

This accelerated movement of Blacks out of the South impinged on the Black woman's reality in very definite ways. Black women migrated North in greater numbers than Black men.[14] Economic necessity dictated that most Black women who migrated to the urban centers find work immediately. In order to survive themselves and to provide for their families, Black women once again found only drudge work available to them. Small numbers of Black women were allowed inside the industrial manufacturing system but were confined to the most tedious, strenuous, and degrading occupations.

> White women had no intentions of working alongside black women; even if some of them did speak of sexual equality, most did not favor racial equality. . . . Fear of competing with blacks as well as the possible loss of job status associated with working with blacks caused white workers to oppose any efforts to have blacks as fellow workers.[15]

The interaction of race and sex in the labor market exacted a heavy toll on the Black woman, making all aspects of migration a problem of paramount religious significance. Her experience as wife and mother, responsible for transmitting the culture, customs, and values of Black community to her children, served as a decisive factor in determining how the Bible was read and understood. At the same time that the Black woman was trying to organize family life according to her traditional roles, the male-dominated industrial society required that she serve as catalyst in the transition process. Her own unfamiliarities and adaptation difficulties had to be repressed because she was responsible for making a home in crowded substandard housing, finding inner-city schools that propagated literacy for her children, and earning enough income to cover the most elementary needs.

The Struggle for Justice

Black religion and the Black church served as a sustaining force, assuring boundless justice. During these stormy times, the Black church tradition renewed hope and spiritual strength, touching these women's lives in all their ramifications, enabling migrant women to carry on in spite of obstacles and opposition. It was the interpretive principle of the Black church that guided Black women in facing life squarely, in acknowledging its raw coarseness. The white elitist attributes of passive gentleness and an enervative delicacy, considered particularly appropriate to womanhood, proved nonfunctional in the pragmatic survival of migrant Black women. Cultivating conventional amenities was not a luxury afforded them. Instead, Black women were aware that their very lives depended upon their being able to decipher the various sounds in the larger world, to hold in check the nightmare figures of terror, to fight for basic freedoms against the sadistic law enforcement agencies in their communities, to resist the temptation to capitulate to the demands of the status quo, to find meaning in the most despotic circumstances, and to create something where nothing existed before. Most of the time this was accompanied by the unceasing mumbling of prayers. "But nothin' never hurt me 'cause de Lawd knowed how it was."[16]

World Wars I and II brought the most visible changes in Black life. Under coercive pressure from the Black community, the federal government was forced to take definite steps to halt discrimination in war industries. With white labor reserves depleted, large numbers of Black women and men were hired. In segregated plants and factories, Black women attained semiskilled, skilled, and supervisory positions. A few were even granted limited rights in auxiliary unions. Most Black women, however, were assigned the most arduous tasks, worked in the least skilled jobs, and received lower wages than their white counterparts.

The biblical teachings of the Black church continued to initiate and envision the fundamental truth claims operative in the community. The ministers' expositions of the biblical faith corresponded to the efficacious ways that the Black community dealt with contingencies in the real-lived context. The scriptures made a significant difference in the notions Blacks used to see and to act in situations that confronted them [46].

For instance, during this period, segregation was still legally maintained in almost every area of social contact, the horrors of lynching became an accepted reality, and blackface minstrel-burlesque shows were used to reinforce the stereotype of Black people as inferior. Black churchwomen became crusaders for justice. They recorded and talked about the grimness of struggle among the least visible people in the society. Given their hostile environment, deteriorating conditions, and the enduring humiliation of the social ostracism of the war years, these women exposed the most serious and unyielding problem of the twentieth century—the single most determining factor of Black existence in America—the question of color.

In the years following the world wars, white mob violence, bloody race riots, and "hate strikes" broke out in northern and southern cities alike. Innocent Blacks were beaten, dragged by vehicles, and forced out of their homes. Substantial amounts of Black-owned property were destroyed. Throughout the country, extralegal barriers resurged to prevent social equality. Lynching, burning, castrating, beating, cross-burning, tarring and feathering, masked night rides, verbal threats, hate rallies, public humiliations, and random discharging of shotguns in windows were all used by white vigilante groups "to shore up the color line."

Blacks served in World War II as soldiers and civilians. Thousands worked in noncombatant labor battalions. All returned home calling for the "double V"—victory abroad and victory at home. Black veterans objected to the second-class treatment traditionally accorded to them. In their cry against the ideological supremacy of racist practices and values, they appealed to the religious heritage of Blacks that began in the invisible church during slavery.

Black Womanist Consciousness

From the period of urbanization of World War II to the present, Black women find that their situation is still a situation of struggle, a struggle to survive collectively and individually against the continuing harsh historical realities and pervasive adversities in today's world. The Korean and Vietnam wars, federal government programs, civil rights movements, and voter-education programs have all had a positive impact on the Black woman's situation, but they have not been able to offset the negative effects of inherent inequities that are inextricably tied to the history and ideological hegemony of racism, sexism, and class privilege.

The Black woman and her family continue to be enslaved to hunger, disease, and the highest rate of unemployment since the Depression of the 1930s. Advances in education, housing, health care, and other necessities that came about during the mid- and late 1960s are deteriorating faster now than ever before. Both in informal day-to-day life and in the formal organizations and institutions in society, Black women are still the victims of the aggravated inequities of the tridimensional phenomenon of race/class/gender oppression. This is the backdrop of the historical context for the emergence of the Black feminist consciousness.

In essence, the Bible is the highest source of authority for most

Black women. In its pages, Black women have learned how to refute the stereotypes that depict Black people as minstrels or vindictive militants, mere ciphers who react only to omnipresent racial oppression. Knowing the Jesus stories of the New Testament helps Black women be aware of the bad housing, overworked mothers, underworked fathers, functional illiteracy, and malnutrition that continue to prevail in the Black community. However, as God-fearing women they maintain that Black life is more than defensive reactions to oppressive circumstances of anguish and desperation. Black life is the rich, colorful creativity that emerged and reemerges in the Black quest for human dignity. Jesus provides the necessary soul for liberation.

Understanding the prophetic tradition of the Bible empowers Black women to fashion a set of values on their own terms, as well as mastering, radicalizing, and sometimes destroying the pervasive negative orientations imposed by the larger society. Also, they articulate possibilities for decisions and action which address forthrightly the circumstances that inescapably color and shape Black life. Black women serve as contemporary prophets, calling other women forth so that they can break away from the oppressive ideologies and belief systems that presume to define their reality.

Black feminist consciousness may be more accurately identified as Black womanist consciousness, to use Alice Walker's concept and definition.[17] As an interpretive principle, the Black womanist tradition provides the incentive to chip away at oppressive structures, bit by bit. It identifies those texts which help Black womanists to celebrate and rename the innumerable incidents of unpredictability in empowering ways. The Black womanist identifies with those biblical characters who hold on to life in the face of formidable oppression. Often compelled to act or to refrain from acting in accordance with the powers and principalities of the external world, Black womanists search the scriptures to learn how to dispel the threat of death in order to seize the present life.

3

Feminist Consciousness and the Interpretation of Scripture

Margaret A. Farley

"When the women returned from the tomb they told all this to the Eleven and to all the others. The women were Mary of Magdala, Joanna, and Mary the mother of James. The other women with them also told the apostles, but this story of theirs seemed pure nonsense, and [the apostles] did not believe them" (Luke 24:9–11, JB). At least one motivation for developing a feminist interpretation of the Christian scriptures is the need that many of us feel to address the question: Is the testimony of these women to be believed; and, if it is, what does it really mean?

What is at stake in developing a feminist hermeneutic—a feminist theory of interpretation—in relation to the Bible is, of course, the interpretation of the biblical witness as a whole. Is it a witness that is life-giving for women and for men, a witness that opens access to some truth that is freeing for all? Is it a witness that enables us to make choices that are authentic and good, that are faithful to the deepest needs of the human community and consonant with its noblest aspirations? Are the women returning from the tomb beguiled by an illusion, used by traditions of which they are a part, adding one more turn to the plot of a story that is only fiction or perhaps even deception or, worse, a story that will serve forever to injure the women who either tell it or hear it?

My aim here is to probe the consequences of feminist consciousness for the interpretation of scripture. I will not attempt to identify the whole of what can be called "feminist consciousness" or begin the task of actual interpretation of scripture. What I will do is try to identify some important elements in feminist consciousness, show how these yield interpretive principles in relation to scripture, and reflect on the function of these for our understanding and use of scripture. In order to set the stage for this, however, I want to consider how feminist consciousness, like any other "consciousness" that includes deeply held convictions about the way things are and ought to be, inevitably and profoundly influences our interpretation of and our belief in the biblical witness [30].

Authority and Content: The Test of "Recognition"

Is the testimony of the women returning from the tomb to be believed? And, if it is, what does it really mean? To put the questions in this way suggests that it is possible to separate them, to separate the question of authenticity, or authority, from the question of content, or meaning. This, however, cannot be done. Herein lies a stumbling block for many who would otherwise like to take seriously a feminist hermeneutic for the Bible. If the question of the authority of the witness is made contingent in any way upon our recognition of the "truth" of its message or the "justice" of its aims, this seems to make of the Bible a secondary source for our knowledge, one that is subject to the test of insights generated from some other more fundamental source. Is this not tantamount to bringing to scripture a test of one's own, a criterion of truth, rather than approaching scripture as a revelatory word, a test of all other claims to truth?

This problem is not easily dismissed, whether a negative or positive resolution is chosen. For many persons, a *recognition* of truth as well as truthfulness is necessary if the Bible is to be a source of life. The authority question is indeed inseparable from the question of content. The reason for this need not be a sophisticated skepticism, certainly not a stiff-necked self-righteousness. It can be, rather, an intuitive or reflective awareness that no communication has real and living power unless it can elicit in us a responding recognition. Call it grace, or previous insight, or a receptivity for truth—unless there is some way in which a new revelation can be recognized by us as true, it cannot free us further from ignorance of falsehood and it cannot awaken us to love.

Massive difficulties are entailed by such an assertion, of course. Qualifications of all kinds may be necessary. I think, however, its plausibility can be shown fairly simply if I treat it for now as a "negative limit." Let me try to explain what I mean by this.

Theologians and ethicists always make some judgments about what sources they will use and how they will use them. For example, they determine that secular disciplines (like philosophy) should be included or excluded as sources for theology; they decide which of their sources takes priority (as when scripture is given priority over the teaching of church leaders); they raise up certain biblical texts and relativize the value of others. Implicit or explicit in these judgments are beliefs about the nature of human understanding, human experience, divine revelation, the authenticity of particular religious traditions, logical consistency, the nature of reality itself. At the heart of such judgments there can be convictions so basic that to contradict them would be to experience violence done to the integrity of the self. The making of such judgments is not unique to theologians and ethicists. It is part of any approach—that of individual believers or whole churches—to the sources of faith and understanding, to discernment of what we can believe and how we are to live what we believe.

My concern here is precisely for the kind of conviction so basic to a person's understanding that a contradictory witness cannot be believed without doing violence to one's self. One can, of course, come to see that the contradictory witness is more true than one's own previous belief. But in this case, it is not violence to the understanding that is experienced. If in such an instance a kind of letting-go of internal barriers to fuller vision is necessary (barriers such as fear of the new or unwillingness to change behavior in accordance with new insights), this does not do violence to our deepest selves, but liberates them. As long as what is presented actually *contradicts* what remain our most fundamental convictions, however, we cannot surrender our minds to it without experiencing violence done to our own integrity.

The biblical witness, on the contrary, claims to present a truth that will heal us, make us whole; it will free us, not enslave us to what violates our very sense of truth and justice. Its appeal to us might be described, in the words of philosopher Paul Ricoeur, as a "nonviolent appeal."[1] As a revelation of truth, it asks for something less like a submission of will and more like an opening of the imagination—and thence the whole mind and heart. In its own terms, then, it cannot be believed unless it rings true to our deepest capacity for truth and goodness. If it contradicts this, it is not to be believed. If it falsifies this, it cannot be accepted [31].

Does this characterization of the biblical witness (that is, that its authority can be acknowledged only if its meaning is perceived as true) risk reducing it to "cheap grace"? Is the Bible really required to answer the demands of reason and the cries of the human heart? It depends, of course, on what one means by the demands of reason and the desires of the human heart. But surely there is a sense in which every religious tradition has power only insofar as it offers just this—insofar as it helps to make sense of the whole of human life, to give meaning to human tragedy and horizons to human hopes. "Hard sayings" can be liberating truths; reason need not be opposed to mystery, nor desire to great-hearted love.

The minimal claim I want to make, however, is that included in feminist consciousness are some fundamental convictions so basic and so important that contradictory assertions cannot be accepted by feminists without violence being done to their very understandings and valuations. These convictions serve as a kind of negative test for any revelation in knowledge. They can serve, too, as a positive key to the fullness of revelation regarding the reality and destiny of human persons. These convictions must, then, function in a feminist interpretation of scripture—discerning the meaning of the biblical witness as a whole and in its parts and thus (though not only thus) whether it is to be believed. Moreover, they serve as principles for selective and interpretive judgments in relation to *all* potential sources for feminist theology and ethics—not only scripture but the history of theology, the comparative study of religions, philosophy, and the sciences, historical events, contemporary social arrangements, and every woman's own experience. If we can identify some of these convictions, it will be possible both to illustrate better their function in a feminist hermeneutic and at the same time to clarify just what a *feminist* hermeneutic may be.

Principles for a Feminist Hermeneutic

Feminist consciousness includes many elements, not all of which are agreed upon by every feminist. There is pluralism within feminism as in any other rich and comprehensive interpretation of humanity and the world. Yet some central convictions are shared at least by large groups of feminists. Most fundamental, perhaps, is the conviction that women are fully human and are to be valued as such. The content of this conviction, however, is different from some similar affirmations that are nonfeminist. Thus, for example, it is not to be mistaken for the view that women are human, though derivatively and partially so. Hence, a feminist belief about the humanness of women is specified by the inclusion of principles of mutuality. Further, feminist consciousness recognizes the importance of women's own experience as a way to understanding; it takes seriously the essential embodiment of human persons; it opens to an ecological view of the value of all of nature and the context of the whole of the universe; it affirms a mode of collaboration as the primary mode for human interaction.

But let me focus somewhat narrowly on the conviction that women are fully human and are to be valued as such. This conviction could well be formulated as the underlying principle for a feminist hermeneutic. In order not to risk trivializing the central insight of feminism, however, it must (as I have already suggested) be understood to include within it at least two closely related principles: (1) the principle of equality (women and men are equally fully human and are to be treated as such) and (2) the principle of mutuality (based on a view of human persons as embodied subjects, essentially relational as well as autonomous and free). In at least one major version of feminism, these are truth claims, founded on a new understanding of the reality of women (and therefore also of men). So profound is their persuasive appeal that they give rise to an experience of a moral imperative. They function, then, as interpretive principles but also as normative ethical principles in a feminist theory of justice. They function, moreover, to ground a strategy of commitment to the well-being of women, to counter whatever biases perpetuate gender inequalities and structural barriers to human mutuality.

Feminists, quite obviously, are not the only persons who have come to convictions about the principles of equality and mutuality. Yet for feminists the content of these principles is not simply equatable with every other articulation of them. It is not the case, for example, that when feminists argue for equality among women and men, they simply extend to women the insights of modern liberal philosophy; or that when feminists raise up the importance of mutuality, they simply repeat the conclusions of theorists of sociality such as George Herbert Mead, Martin Buber, and John Macmurray. Feminists have, of course, learned from all these sources. But they also know that no other tradition or movement has adequately addressed the situation of women. This is not just a failure of extension. Rather, it represents a fundamental need for deeper analysis of the contexts of human life, concepts of the human self, categories of human relation. It makes clear the urgency for taking account of the experience of all groups of human persons. From the interpretive vantage point of the experience of women—of our oppression and our achievements, our needs and our contributions, our freedom and our responsibilities—feminism assumes ground-breaking work on questions of human dignity and models of human relationships. It also assumes transformative experiences of new and growing insight on the part of individuals, deeply formed convictions about the capabilities and possibilities of each human being [28, 38].

Equality

Contemporary feminist consciousness, developed through a careful listening to women's own experience (largely prompted by new

modes of sharing this experience), incorporates certain conclusions. First, all efforts to justify the inferiority of women to men
falsify women's experience. Traditional warrants for gender inequality have been demystified and rejected; women have recognized
the contradiction between received interpretations of our identity
and function on the one hand and our own experience of ourselves
and our lives on the other.

Women have also unmasked deceptive theories that assert a principle of equality but still assume basic inequalities among persons
determined by gender, or race, or any property of individuals and
groups not essential to their humanity as such. Thus, the long-
standing formal principle of equal treatment for equals has been
recognized by women in its radical powerlessness by itself to discern
who are the "equals." Further, where "equal protection under the
law" was said to apply to all persons, women learned only too well
that this did not necessarily include them, just as it did not apply to
slaves. And strong theories of "complementarity" have been exposed that cover for patterns of inequality—for relationships in
which the role of one partner is always inferior to, dependent upon,
instrumental to the role of the other.

Feminist consciousness opens, then, to acknowledge for women
those essential features of personhood that modern liberal philosophy identified for human persons as such: individual autonomy and
a capacity for free choice. Once these features are appropriated for
women as well as men, the conclusion follows that women, too,
must be respected as "ends," not as mere "means." And their
interests and aims must be respected no less than men's.

Equitable Sharing

But women have learned more from their experience than the
lessons of liberal philosophy. Their own experience of disadvan-
tage, and their perception of the disadvantaged histories of others
who are similarly fully human, have impelled a feminist universaliza-
tion of the principle of equality that includes a claim by all to an
equitable share in the goods and services necessary to human life
and basic happiness. The accumulated experience of life situations
in which inequality is not limited to political powerlessness or personal lack of esteem but is a matter of hunger and homelessness,
sickness and injury, has pushed feminist consciousness to a positive
form of the principle of equality—one based not only on the self-
protective right of each to freedom but on the positive, self-yield-
ing as well as self-enhancing, participation of all in human solidarity.

Mutuality

Finally, then, women have found in their experience clear indications of the inadequacy of a view of human persons that respects them by isolating them one from another. When autonomy is the sole basis of human dignity and the single principle for social arrangements, individuals are atomized. Their primary mode of relating becomes one of opposition and competition between the self and the other. Women claim that gross forms of individualism not only undermine the common good but fail to take account of another essential feature of personhood—the feature of relationality, that feature which ultimately requires mutuality as the primary goal of relationships between persons [144].

Only with a principle of mutuality can human persons truly be affirmed as embodied subjects; as beings whose value lies not only in their freedom but also in their capacity to know and be known, to love and be loved; as beings whose destiny is communion.

Deep in women's experience lies the long-standing awareness of the reality that theorists of sociality have come to see. Feminist consciousness stands as a corrective to a liberal philosophy that fails to understand human solidarity and the importance and need for mutuality. But it also stands as a corrective to theories of sociality that fail to incorporate a requirement for basic human equality; that fail to affirm the feature of autonomy along with the feature of relationality. Feminists thus reject romantic returns to organic models of society where woman's relation is determined, each in her own place, without regard for free agency or for personal identity and worth that transcend roles. Yet feminists are convinced that persons, women and men, are centers of life, capable (without contradiction) of being centered more and more in themselves as they are centered more and more beyond themselves in one another. They are convinced, too, that in this mystery of autonomy and relationality, equality and mutuality, lie the clues we need for the relation of persons to the whole universe in which we live. But what can these convictions, and the principles that express them, mean for the interpretation and use of the biblical witness?

Feminist Interpretation of Scripture

The need for interpretation of scripture is clear. Without interpretation, we are not able to believe the witness that is presented. This is not only because there is reason to be suspicious of scripture, but because without interpretation we are not able to "hear" what was spoken in another time, to understand its meaning for us. In

this, contemporary feminists are not unique. The necessity for interpretation exists for all those who struggle to know what was written
in another context, who ask whether a tradition is living in which
they can stand. This does not mean that no one can experience a
present direct address through the mediation of scripture, but even
the immediacy of such experience is not free of the need for interpretation—interpretation of the experience and what is encoun-
tered in it. Interpretation of sacred scriptures from *within* the tradition for which they are scriptures, and sacred, is precisely the
bringing together of the horizons of a far-reaching tradition and
present life situations. For Christians the task of interpretation has
been under way from the beginning—as, for example, when a New
Testament hermeneutic was addressed to the Old Testament, and
when Paul interpreted the story of Jesus in relation to the lives of
the early churches, and when in each century there was acknowledged the need to hear and hear again.[2]

For those who are reluctant to bring to scripture what seems to
be a measure for its meaning and authority, one solution suggests
itself in the face of a seeming dilemma. That is, it might be argued
that scripture itself provides the basis for feminist consciousness.
True discernment of the biblical witness yields feminist insights,
which in turn become principles of interpretation for the rest of
scripture. In other words, convictions regarding the full humanity
of women emerge precisely from the bringing of women's experience to the address of scripture.

The difficulty with attributing solely to scripture the genesis of
feminist consciousness is that it seems clearly contrary to fact. Not
all feminists have come to their beliefs about the reality of women,
about equality and mutuality, simply by reading the Bible. Some, at
least, have come to these convictions influenced by the intellectual
history of our civilization, by the cultural milieu which this intellectual history has helped to form, by the changes in women's own
lives, by the sharing of women's recognition of contradictions between received traditions and their own experience. Insight into
women's reality may be prompted for some by encounter with biblical texts, confirmed and expanded for others, left untouched for still
others, contradicted for others still. Within the potential religious
experience of women, the fundamental question is not whether
original vision is generated by scripture but how, given this vision,
scripture is to be approached.

Some fairly standard ways in which Christian ethicists think about
scripture as a source can be helpful to us here. For example, most
Christian ethicists would not claim that the Bible (or Christian theology, for that matter) provides exclusive access to moral insight.[3]

Scripture is indeed a source for Christian ethics in a variety of ways. It can reveal moral principles, ideals, guidelines, values. It can aid moral discernment by illuminating the human condition, possibilities of human agency, obstacles to moral goodness. It can motivate moral action by making present a divine promise and call, a history of people formed in faith, a glimpse of what is to be hoped for. It can empower persons religiously and morally by mediating a fundamental meaning for their lives, stretching them always beyond themselves, challenging self-deception, enabling self-acceptance. But in all of this, the Bible may not yield very specific moral rules or action guides, and the general principles it offers may have no ready application to contemporary life. Without other sources of moral wisdom, the power of scripture cannot be mediated into the contemporary context.

On this basis can we ask, then, what it might mean to acknowledge the authority of scripture as a source for Christian and feminist faith, theology, ethics? First, it is helpful to be clear about what it does *not* mean (or at least need not mean, within a traditionally recognized pluralism of approaches by Christians to scripture). It does not mean that some important insights—regarding life, morality, even hope—cannot come both from the Bible and from other sources, or only from other sources. It does not mean, moreover, that scripture is sufficient in itself for the development of a wholly adequate Christian feminist theology or ethic.

Positively, what it *can* mean for feminists to acknowledge the authority of scripture as a source for understanding human persons and human life is that (1) at least scripture contains something more than a patriarchal view of human life, a support for sexism, and (2) the "more" that scripture embodies rings at least in harmony with the truth of women's reality as it is understood in feminist consciousness—touches it, perhaps unfolds it, makes it resonate with other truths, perhaps can help to test fidelity to it. For those for whom scripture has this authority, the interpretive task becomes imperative [146].

We must ask more specifically, however, in what way feminist consciousness can function in the interpretation of scripture. I have already said that principles of a feminist hermeneutic will serve first as a negative limit. It may be clearer now what it means to say that deep convictions, when they are brought to the interpretation of scripture or any other source for faith, for theology, for ethics, serve precisely as a negative limit. Whatever contradicts those convictions cannot be accepted as having the authority of an authentic revelation of truth. It is simply a matter of there being no turning back. We can be dispossessed of our best insights, proven wrong in our judgments. But as long as those insights continue to make sense to us, and as long as our basic judgments seem to us incontrovertible, there can be no turning back. So it is with feminist consciousness and the interpretation of scripture.

Feminists quite readily acknowledge the historical nature of human knowledge and the social nature of the interpretation of human experience. Yet feminist consciousness is experienced as an immeasurable advance over the false consciousness it replaces or the implicit consciousness it renders explicit. Scales have fallen from persons' eyes, and they cannot be put back. The fact that present insights are still partial, that present formulations of principles may change, that the meaning of principles can vary significantly from context to context—none of this changes the requirement that new understandings must be tested for truth (for accuracy and adequacy) against the reality of women's lives as revealed in women's experience. It is no fancy, no illusion, that feminists believe they bring to the interpretation of scripture.

If, within the negative limit, the biblical witness as a whole is experienced as authentic—if, in other words, some religious authority is given to scripture—then the interpretive task remains in relation to all the parts of the whole. That is, insofar as scripture is judged by feminists to be a source for faith, for theology, ethics, and life, then the negative limit also functions in discerning the meaning of specific texts, specific aspects of the biblical story. On the basis of feminist convictions, then, some interpretations are ruled out (just as an overall acceptance of the love commandment as central to Christian life and to the teaching of scripture rules out final interpretations that contradict it). Thus, for example, a divine imperative which universalizes a requirement that women fill inferior roles is ruled out as the final word of the biblical witness [36]. Different feminist interpreters will rule out such interpretations in different ways, of course. Within a pluralism of approaches, some will deny the validity of texts that hold such content; some will relativize the importance of such texts; some will interpret the texts under a feminist paradigm that makes them negative symbols of what the overall witness is portraying [132].

But, as I have said, feminist principles of interpretation serve more than as a negative limit in discerning the meaning of scripture. Insofar as scripture is believed to shed light on human experience, feminist interpretive principles must function to probe its stories and its teachings, its poetry and its oracles, searching for positive clues for the ongoing task of finding meaning and making decisions in our concrete lives (just as the love commandment sets questions for discernment, searching for analogies between the tradition and the lives of those who approach the tradition). New questions are themselves principles of movement in understanding. It is possible that a feminist hermeneutic can allow more scales to drop from our eyes, so that the biblical witness is freed for our seeing in a way that must otherwise remain forever obscured.

Two final observations may be in order. When an interpretive principle rises out of experience that is importantly characterized by oppression and suffering, it carries with it a moral imperative for use. Feminists must approach scripture, and every other source of religious faith and practice, with hermeneutical principles that not only render the sources accessible to feminist consciousness but more and more inaccessible for the harmful aims of sexism. Whatever problems its writers had in attaining anything like a feminist consciousness, they knew well the tragic fact that persons "hear and hear, but do not understand; see and see, but do not perceive" (Isa. 6:9). Thus was their own task set. Thus, too, is set the task of feminist interpretation for a long time to come.

Last of all, it may not be nonsense to suggest that feminists have powerful reasons to hope that the women returning from the tomb bear a witness that is life-giving and that can help to deepen and widen every understanding of life and destiny. Human persons need, after all, an ongoing word to meet the word in our hearts. We need religious symbols whose power is a power of access to reality; a promise that can allow us to risk basic trust in life and the world; a call that can help us to be faithful to the truth we hold. We need, also, to acknowledge an essential human openness to any sacred truth and any sacred presence. If the story of the women is to be believed, it will do more than pass a critical test. It will do more than reveal new meaning. Feminists can know the risks—but also the inestimable hope—of giving these women a hearing.

Part II

Feminists at Work

4

Feminist Uses
of Biblical Materials

Katharine Doob Sakenfeld

As a Christian who teaches the Bible and who also calls herself a feminist, I am often asked, "How can feminists use the Bible, if at all? What approach to the Bible is appropriate for feminists who locate themselves within the Christian community? How does the Bible serve as a resource for Christian feminists?" These are not easy questions to answer, but it is possible to identify several different ways in which contemporary Christian feminists approach the biblical material. This chapter describes some of these ways of listening to the Bible.

Feminism may be viewed as a contemporary prophetic movement that announces judgment on the patriarchy of contemporary culture and calls for repentance and change. How does such a prophetic movement relate itself to its religious heritage? The prophets of the Hebrew scriptures sometimes highlighted forgotten traditions of ancient Israel; on other occasions, they found it necessary to reinterpret traditions that had been skewed or misunderstood; at times they even had to reject time-honored traditions as false in their understanding of God's way. Christian feminists who intend and hope, like the biblical prophets, to work within their religious heritage must address themselves to the authority of the Bible in the life of their community of faith. They must seek faithful ways of recovering, reinterpreting, and discerning God's way in the tradition handed on in the Bible [119].

Their beginning point, shared in common with all feminists studying the Bible, is appropriately a stance of radical suspicion. In chapter 7 in this volume, Drorah Setel illustrates this way of beginning from radical suspicion as undertaken by a Jewish feminist. Feminists recognize in common that patriarchy was one of the most stable features of ancient biblical society over the thousand-plus years of the Bible's composition and redaction. Thus, in studying any biblical texts, feminists need to be alert not only for explicit patriarchal bias but also for evidence of more subtle androcentrism in the worldview of the biblical authors. Only such a frank and often painful assessment of the depth of patriarchal perspective in the text provides an honest starting point for considering how the tradition can be meaningful today. If in studying a text feminists discover that some suspicions are unfounded, then there is cause for rejoicing, but in the meantime they have not fooled themselves by refusing to face the problem [86].

Recognizing the patriarchy of biblical materials, Christian feminists approach the text with at least three different emphases:

1. Looking to texts about women to counteract famous texts used "against" women.

2. Looking to the Bible generally (not particularly to texts about women) for a theological perspective offering a critique of patriarchy (some may call this a "liberation perspective").

3. Looking to texts about women to learn from the intersection of history and stories of ancient and modern women living in patriarchal cultures.

These emphases are not presented as the only possibilities but rather as major categories identifiable in current feminist biblical interpretation. Before I describe them, two important points should be noted about their interrelationship.

First, these three approaches represent options. They do not necessarily occur as a series of stages in the life of a feminist struggling with the biblical text, nor do they represent a chronological history of feminist biblical interpretation generally. One may move from one approach to another in the order described here, but one may also enter into feminist dialogue with the Bible beginning with any one of these approaches. Feminist interpretation moves back and forth among these options.

Second, these three options are not actually mutually exclusive. Many general essays on feminism and the Bible incorporate some combination of them. Some interpreters use different approaches on different occasions, depending on the purpose and the audience. Thus it is important not to associate individual feminists simplistically with just one of these options. Readers are invited to consider what combinations of these options they find in the next four chapters of this volume.

Option 1: Looking to Texts About Women to Counteract Famous Texts Used "Against" Women

The various ways in which the Bible has been and is still used to justify women's traditional place in Western culture have been recounted many times over. Texts and traditions used to bolster the cultural status quo include (among many others) the themes that woman was created second (Genesis 2) and sinned first (Genesis 3 and the reinforcement of this view in 1 Tim. 2:13–14); that women must keep silent in church (1 Cor. 14; 1 Tim. 2); and that they should be submissive to their husbands (Ephesians 5). Feminism as a prophetic movement identifies such texts, or the traditional interpretation of them, as "against" women. Within option 1, feminists offer a twofold response: on the one hand, there is an effort to reinterpret some of these well-known texts; on the other hand, "forgotten" texts that present women in a different light are brought into the discussion.

So, for example, a number of studies of Genesis 2—3 have suggested fresh interpretations that are not so negative toward women. The creation of woman at the end of chapter 2 may in fact mean that she is equal to the man; in the encounter with the serpent, the woman and the man should be viewed as "mutually responsible," united in disobedience. In a similar vein, New Testament specialists point out that Paul's instruction for women to keep silent (1 Cor. 14) is advice peculiar to a disruptive situation in the church at Corinth. The discussion of marriage in Ephesians 5 is often treated by emphasizing the theme of mutual subjection of verse 21, which introduces the section [104–105].

Complementary to such reinterpretation of negatively viewed passages is a new emphasis on those texts which seem to speak positively of women. Galatians 3:28 is surely the parade example: "There is neither Jew nor Greek, there is neither slave nor free, there is neither male nor female; for you are all one in Christ Jesus." Many Christian feminists ground their view of women's place in family, society, and church on this text, which for them points beyond the generally restrictive practice of the early church and applies to actual living in the world, not simply to personal salvation.

Feminists have also turned to the many stories of Jesus' relationship to women as recorded in the Gospels and to the scattered indications of women in leadership roles that are treated with approval in scripture. The role and actions of biblical characters such as Miriam, Deborah, the women at Jesus' tomb, Priscilla, and many

others are treated paradigmatically to suggest that women may assume leadership and authority in their communities. Jesus' attitude
toward women (speaking with them, taking them seriously) is regarded as exceptional and even revolutionary for his time—an attitude which then informs a critique of patriarchy both in the early
church and today [70]. The story of Jesus' encounter with the Samaritan woman at the well (John 4) is often drawn upon: Jesus first
announces his messiahship to this symbolic outcast of society—a
woman of questionable repute who is also a Samaritan.

This first option—using reinterpreted or forgotten texts about
women to counteract texts used "against" women—has its own
strengths and limitations. Some of these will be described briefly.
Readers are encouraged to reflect on the implications of these for
the passages just mentioned or for other texts about women in
which they have special interest.

A great strength of this approach, in my view, lies in drawing our
attention to the diversity of biblical testimony concerning women,
by its recovery of forgotten positive texts and traditions. The very
existence of such potentially positive material suggests that the
Bible is not necessarily to be rejected out of hand as an instrument
of patriarchy. At the same time, the reinterpretation of allegedly
negative texts serves as reminder of the ongoing power of patriarchy in biblical interpretation. The reinterpretations, by their
very existence, challenge the claim that exegesis is scientifically
factual and value-neutral. The prophetic tasks of recovery and reinterpretation work together to suggest that some parts of the traditional Christian view of women may be false.

But in this strength lurks also a potential limitation. The assumptions which sometimes underlie this option are that the Bible has
some clear and explicit teaching concerning the status and role of
women, that the locus of this teaching is in texts specifically concerning women, and that it may be (re-)discovered by careful exegetical study. Yet the reinterpretations of texts used against
women certainly have not gained universal acceptance. A single
agreed-upon methodology yields radically different conclusions in
the hands of different exegetes. How is a feminist to deal with the
absence of exegetical agreement concerning many, if not all, of the
critical passages under discussion? Given the assumption that careful exegesis of texts about women will yield a sure answer about
women's proper role in church and culture, the lack of interpretive
consensus undermines the very purpose for which many feminists
use this approach.

Furthermore, if there remain some negative texts concerning
women for which no reinterpretation seems possible (and surely

such do remain), what principle of discernment decides which set of texts is authoritative? How does one choose between texts that uphold the status quo and texts that challenge it? Although most careful studies try to suggest some principle (such as New Testament over Hebrew scriptures; Jesus over Paul; eternally valid statements over culture-bound statements), the person struggling with the issue often perceives the situation simply as one in which competing proof texts are at work. Galatians 3:28 is tossed into the ring to compete with 1 Timothy 2, and no real headway is made. And of course any of the principles of discernment just mentioned raise other serious problems, in suggesting that some parts of the Bible are more trustworthy than others or in implying that some biblical material may not be culture-bound.

Each of these two main areas of limitation—exegetical uncertainty and competing proof-texting—points to basic questions about the meaning of biblical authority and the usefulness of the Bible for Christian faith. These questions will be addressed briefly at the conclusion of this chapter.

Option 2: Looking to the Bible Generally for a Theological Perspective Offering a Critique of Patriarchy

This approach does not set out to avoid texts mentioning women but, unlike the first option, it does not focus upon such texts as the sole or even primary basis for developing a Christian perspective on the role and status of women. It approaches the Bible in the hope of recognizing what the gospel is really all about and then works from that recognition toward a specificity about women.

At the most general level, this option is illustrated by the understanding of the Bible as words that bear witness to the incarnate Word of God, Jesus Christ. This view of scripture suggests that the Bible is not an instruction book but that the test of any situation would be an understanding of God's way with the world made known in Jesus of Nazareth. The problem, of course, within this option is to discern some central witness of scripture that can be identified as what Christianity is all about.[1] Feminist efforts in this direction tend to set their reflection within the larger context of liberation theology.

Letty Russell, for example, emphasizes the theme of *koinonia* as partnership and the many ways in which people are partners together in God's liberating action. To live out this partnership, she suggests, Christians need to develop the "art of anticipation" so that they may think from the context of God's future, discern the signs of liberation, and act on the basis of that hope. It is by such theological anticipation that feminists see "both male and female in community as God's intention for New Creation." This New Creation perspective is grounded in Jesus Christ as Prince of Shalom and witnessed to in the biblical traditions of unexpected deliverance from oppression and unexpected establishment of a new covenant. God's horizon is always out ahead of people, challenging them to transform their worldview [139–140].[2]

Rosemary Ruether's chapter entitled "Biblical Resources for Feminism: The Prophetic Principles" in her book *Sexism and God Talk* provides a second illustration of this approach. For Ruether, the prophetic principles "imply a rejection of every elevation of one social group against others as image and agent of God, every use of God to justify social domination and subjugation" [116–119].[3] In Ruether's view the application of this prophetic message of liberation must be pressed beyond the content of the Bible itself in order to apply it to women. Old Testament Israel, imbued with patriarchy, simply never noticed that women were among those oppressed and in need of liberation. And despite first-century Christian glimpses of a transformed relationship between women and men, the early church quashed nascent change in this direction. Ruether's approach involves regarding the "egalitarian, countercultural vision" (which must be read between the lines of the New Testament) as the "true norm of Christianity [so that] the authority of the official canonical framework is overturned."[4]

In common, Ruether and Russell look to the biblical message overall, not in the first place to texts about women. The range of biblical texts appropriate to the task thus conceived is wide indeed. Possibilities range from the exodus to the jubilee year, to Zacchaeus, to the abundant life, to Paul on freedom.

One great strength of this approach is that it can look beyond the reactive side of feminism as antipatriarchalism and move to (even start from) the more positive and constructive side of feminist emphasis on *shalom,* wholeness or salvation in the broadest and deepest sense of the term. Because this *shalom* encompasses all people, both women and men, in all conditions of life (race, ethnicity, class), this option puts feminist use of biblical materials concretely in touch with the concerns and quests of other oppressed groups. It provides a basis for affirming the solidarity of the whole human community and for questioning any arbitrary prioritizing of the needs of one group over another. The attempt to start from an understanding of "what the Christian thing is all about" (gospel as humanization; prophetic critique of oppression) also has the advantage of reminding us that each particular biblical passage takes on meaning in the light of many others. The range of texts offering good news for women is vastly expanded by comparison to option 1.

But as with option 1, so here also strength is at the same time limitation. "The gospel" is very general, and for many people encounter with the general message of Christianity is vague and diffuse by comparison to encounter with specific texts. And when this option turns to consider specific texts, the encounter with the liberation theme in general may still be experienced as diffuse despite its application to the condition of women.

Elisabeth Schüssler Fiorenza has pointed to two other potential limitations of this option.[5] While they are not in my view inherent in the approach, they do represent concerns that should be considered by those focusing on this option [131–132].

First, this approach runs the risk of concealing patriarchy in the biblical witness itself. Those who use this option are quick to agree that radical suspicion is necessary and that the whole Bible is infused with patriarchy. In fact, they use this option in part because they do see patriarchal bias even in the many texts about women that can be remembered or reinterpreted to challenge the status quo. And yet there is a danger that the patriarchal character of the liberation texts as they were written will be forgotten. Ruether's radicalizing of the biblical critique of oppression to include women would then be lost, and one would fall into the false assumption that biblical authors speaking against oppression had in mind women as well as other oppressed groups [118].

A second limitation lies in the possible claim that there is some timeless or eternal truth to be identified in scripture, while all the actual writers and texts fall short of that truth. Indeed, for many people this is precisely the assumption underlying this second option, so that their goal in using this approach is to shuck off the culturally conditioned parts of the Bible and find that timeless truth. But many who work from this assumption discover that seeking for something free of historical conditioning is like peeling an onion: There is no core. I do not find that either Russell or Ruether, carefully read, succumbs to this peeling-the-onion approach, although I appreciate Fiorenza's concern. To identify key elements of a tradition is not necessarily to remove the tradition from the context in which it was hammered out, but avoiding this consequence requires deliberate attention to the problem.

Again, as with option 1, the limitations of option 2 call into question the ultimate usefulness of the biblical materials and direct our attention to issues of authority.

Option 3: Looking to Texts About Women to Learn
from the History and Stories
of Ancient and Modern Women
Living in Patriarchal Cultures

I have tried to state this third option to open up in principle any biblical text dealing with women as one that can have meaning for modern feminists. In contrast to option 1, in which texts about women are categorized as for or against women, in this third option all these texts are taken to address the condition of women as persons oppressed because of their sex and as persons yearning to be free. Within this option it does not ultimately matter whether a given text can be proved exegetically to support feminist concerns. It does not matter because here the Bible is not (in contrast to option 1) looked to as a source of direct and specific rules for living. Rather, the Bible is viewed as an instrument by which God shows women their true condition as people who are oppressed and yet who are given a vision of a different heaven and earth and a variety of models for how to live toward that vision.[6] The work of two biblical specialists who make use of very different exegetical styles and skills also illustrates this option.

Phyllis Trible's *Texts of Terror* gives close literary attention to narratives portraying women as victims, some of whom nonetheless find ways to declare their personhood. Trible describes this task as retelling biblical stories of terror *in memoriam*. She interprets the story of the rape, murder, and dismemberment of an unnamed woman (Judges 19), the story of a daughter offered as human sacrifice because of her father's foolish vow (Judges 11), and other stories "on behalf of their female victims in order to recover a neglected history, to remember a past that the present embodies, and to pray that these terrors shall not come to pass again."[7]

A historical rather than literary focus characterizes Elisabeth Schüssler Fiorenza's contribution within the scope of this third option. As a historian of earliest Christianity, she seeks to reconstruct the life and practice of Christians and congregations in the earliest church. In this task she examines New Testament texts against women not in order to rehabilitate them (as in option 1) but rather to reconstruct the practices that the New Testament authors were rejecting so as to clarify our picture of church life in the New Testament period and to describe women's role in that church life. Recognizing that the Bible is thoroughly androcentric, recorded and canonized by men, Fiorenza moves the locus of revelation beyond the text itself to the reconstructed ministry of Jesus and the life of the early church, in which at every stage the picture is one of "struggle for equality and against patriarchal domination."[8]

Despite significant differences in critical method and in presupposition about the place of the biblical text in the life of the church, both Trible and Fiorenza are focusing on the "intersection of history and stories of ancient and modern women living in patriarchal cultures." One strength common to their work is the possibility of facing the pervasive androcentrism of the biblical material head on, without excuse or evasion. Women may appropriate the tradition by identifying with biblical women both in their oppression and in their exercise of freedom.

Yet, like the other options, this one too has its limitation as it brings its user up against the question of authority. How does one know that, insofar as a text perpetuates violence and oppression against women (or against anyone), it is in that respect not authoritative? The problem is that, for option 3, the discernment of what is authoritative must come from somewhere outside the option itself, whether from biblical reflection done from the perspective of option 2, or from the personal and communal experience of the person approaching the text, or perhaps most fruitfully from some combination of these.

To Give Up on the Bible—
or to Understand Its Authority in a New Way?

Whichever option they find most congenial, Christian feminists sometimes assume that if they use the Bible in that particular way, patriarchy will be undone in their own lives; and that if enough others follow their use of the Bible, patriarchy will disappear. But if and when they find that the systemic pervasiveness of patriarchy is such that patriarchy will not disappear in their lifetime or even in the next generation, then attention to the Bible begins to seem futile, for the Bible is no longer seen as the key to "solving the problem" of patriarchy. Indeed, the continuing power of the Bible to support the patriarchal status quo underlines its seeming uselessness. With the question "Why would God let such a book become the church's book?" these women and men begin to give up on Christian faith as well.

In addition to this general reason for giving up on the Bible, each of the three options may lead in its own way to rejection of the Bible as not authoritative or not useful in any positive way for the feminist struggle.

The person who comes to see option 1 as merely a proof-texting game may well conclude that the Bible cannot function normatively if it disagrees with itself. The recognition that expert scholars cannot agree on the meaning or significance of given texts will serve only to reinforce this conclusion. To make the Bible worth using, some new conception of authority would need to be offered that could replace the old assumptions about the function of the Bible in the life of faith.

Similarly, with option 2, the Bible's minimal and marginal critique of patriarchy itself may become a stumbling block. What warrant is there, someone will ask, for extending the Bible's general critique of oppression to a critique of patriarchy that is not in the text and seems even to be counterindicated by much of the text? Or the Bible's general attitude toward women may appear so incongruous in light of the central gospel witness to Jesus Christ that the very usefulness of the Bible is thereby called into question.

Finally, option 3 may also lead to abandonment of the Bible as not useful. In this option, the explicit emphasis on the depth and continuity of patriarchy simply highlights the many painfully oppressive portions of biblical material and makes clear that the church has often perpetuated precisely those oppressive emphases. The undercurrent of women living freed and freeing lives within the context of patriarchy has always remained just that—only an undercurrent. In the face of such overwhelming patriarchy, how can one say that this undercurrent should rightly be viewed as the mainstream of the good news of God? Unless feminists find some understanding of how women's rejected history and untold story can be regarded as authoritative, even those using this third approach may in the end give up on the Bible.

Thus no feminist use of biblical material is finally immune to the risk of finding the Bible hurtful, unhelpful, not revealing of God, and not worth the effort to come to grips with it. Regardless of approach, feminists may find that the Bible seems to drive them away from itself (and sometimes from God), rather than drawing them closer. At the heart of the problem lies the issue of biblical authority. The chapters in Part III will provide further discussion of this critical issue.

5

A Gentile Woman's Story

Sharon H. Ringe

The church has trouble with uppity women. Such women are co-opted, ridiculed, ignored, condemned—one way or another gotten out of the way of the important business of the church and of theology. The Gentile woman whose story is told in Mark 7:24–30 and Matthew 15:20–28 has been dealt with in all these ways at various times in the church's history and in modern critical and theological interpretation. This study is presented *in memoriam*[1]—in memory of her and of her fate and for the encouragement of her sisters.

The church has trouble with uppity women. Like the woman in this story, they have shown a knack for confronting pretense, predictability, and easy solutions when these are presented as a way of domesticating the offense and liberating the power of the gospel. This study is presented in celebration of the gifts and ministry of this woman and for the encouragement of her sisters.

The anonymous woman in this story comes across at first and second glance as an uppity woman. She is depicted as interrupting Jesus' rest (Mark) and annoying the disciples (Matthew). She is shown pursuing her request for help from Jesus by a verbal sparring match worthy of the craftiest of teachers (a role explicitly denied to women in Jesus' society). She even wins the argument and is said in the short run to have obtained the healing of her daughter and in the long run to have opened the way for Jesus' (and the church's) mission beyond the Jewish community.

The longer I spent with this story, coming to know and to befriend the woman in the context of the church that continues to tell her story, the more perplexed I became. I found myself cheering the woman for her gutsiness, wit, and self-possession, and at the same time I was offended at the picture of Jesus that the story presents. I wanted to know where such a scandalous story came from, how it found its way into the Gospels, and what point it made for those who told and retold the story and for those who heard it in the church.

The disciplines of biblical criticism have taught me to approach those questions by working backward through the stories as they are presented in the Gospels, much like peeling away the layers of an onion. The problem I met, however, was that working through the disciplines of source, form, and redaction criticism led to treating the text like an onion, whose bite and flavor is in the layers but which has no core, as Katharine Sakenfeld points out in chapter 4. I learned from those layers, and from the process of examining them, how the church has adapted the story to its ecclesiastical needs and, more generally, how we who are the insiders of the church and the privileged of society work to domesticate the gospel to our point of view and to protect the Christ who is familiar and safe from the Christ who offends us. But the formal disciplines of biblical criticism left me on my own just when the only place to move was into the crucible of the story, where its power to confront and to transform could begin to work.

I invite you to journey with me, through the church's struggle to find a place for this story in its gospel and across the bridge of those questions that traditional disciplines and church interpretation leave unanswered. Finally, I invite you to enter with me into the woman's story, there to learn from her about the Christ and so also about God and about ourselves.

The Evangelists' Agenda: The Critical Task

Matthew and Mark set their similar versions of this story in or near the Gentile territory around Tyre and Sidon.[2] The two accounts differ in the point of view from which the story is told and in the relative emphasis given to the healing of the woman's daughter and to the dialogue between the woman and Jesus. In Mark a narrator sets the stage and tells us of the daughter's illness, the mother's request for Jesus to perform an exorcism, and the woman's witnessing of the successful cure. The sharp exchange between them ends in a blessing (of sorts) for the woman and in Jesus' recognition of the daughter's healing. In Matthew we are led into the event by an extended dialogue, instead of being informed about it by a narrator's report. Although Matthew uses both additions to and adaptions of the brief dialogue in Mark's account to develop his interpretation of the incident (such as by portraying the woman's reply to Jesus as less direct and perhaps more submissive),[3] the impression we get is that we are learning about the incident from the woman, the disciples, and Jesus directly. The result is that in Matthew there is less emphasis on the exorcism itself and more on the interaction of the characters.

Several details suggest that Matthew's account has been influenced by other portions of the gospel tradition and represents a reworking of the Markan story. First of all, this story and the story of the healing of the centurion's servant (Matt. 8:5–13; Luke 7:1–10) have several points in common. Both stories have to do with Gentiles, both depict Jesus at a distance from the person who is healed, and both mention the "faith" of one of the characters. In both stories, Matthew's versions present more extended dialogues than are found in the parallel accounts, and in both cases the dialogues have to do with participation in the reign of God. Matthew's story of the healing of two blind men (Matt. 20:29–34), which parallels the story of Bartimaeus in Mark 10:46–52, may also have influenced Matthew's version of the story of the Gentile woman, since both stories tell of a rebuke of the petitioners by onlookers, and in both the petitioners address Jesus as *kyrios* (which carries the double meaning of a polite "sir" and the confessional title "Lord" or "Sovereign") and as "Son of David."

Figuring out the form of the story, and consequently the role it played in the church before being incorporated into the Gospel, presents several difficulties. On the surface it appears to be a story of an exorcism, expanded by a controversy dialogue. Thus, following Mark's account, we are told of the severity of the child's illness (v. 25a) and of the earnestness of the mother's efforts to obtain help for her (vs. 25b, 26b) and the fact that the exorcism has indeed taken place (v. 30). The dialogue between Jesus and the mother comes at the place where we expect the means of healing to be disclosed. The absence of that detail (which Matthew supplies in v. 28b of his account), plus the coherence of the Markan story as a dramatic setting for the exchange between Jesus and the woman,[4] lead some scholars to suggest that this is therefore primarily a "pronouncement story" and specifically (with Bultmann) a "controversy dialogue," built around the sayings in verses 27–28.[5] However, that suggestion too presents a problem, because the exchange between Jesus and the woman reverses the pattern usually found in such stories. Usually a situation or event provokes a hostile question from some onlooker to Jesus, to which Jesus responds with a correcting or reproving question and then drives home his point by a concluding statement which the opponent would be hard put to deny. In this story, however, it is Jesus who provides the hostile saying and the woman whose retort trips him up and corrects him. It is hard to imagine why the church at any stage of its development would want to present the Christ it confesses in such a light!

Many scholars rely on Mark's editorial placement of this story in the Gospel, supported by the fact that there is indeed evidence that in Jewish tradition Gentiles were called "dogs,"[6] to account for the existence of this story in the church's lore about Jesus and even to legitimate the portrait of Jesus it presents. These scholars suggest that the story is to be understood in the context of the early church's struggle to comprehend the Gentile mission and subsequent relationship between Jews and Gentiles in the church and in God's agenda of salvation. This story would address such an ecclesiastical situation by grounding the solution to these problems in the remembered ministry of Jesus. Indeed, the place where Mark has incorporated this story into the Gospel does suggest that he intended it to address the expansion of the limits of the community of faith. The episodes in Mark 6:45—8:26 portray Jesus not only in and around Gentile territory and encountering Gentile people but also dealing with the principal issue in Jewish-Gentile relations: namely, the issue of defilement (Mark 7:1–23). These stories mirror many earlier episodes of Jesus' ministry reportedly carried out in Jewish territory.[7] Following the cycle of stories among the Gentiles is the story of the incident at Caesarea Philippi, which appears to seal Jesus' fate and to propel the Gospel to its inevitable conclusion in Jerusalem. In this context, the story of the Gentile woman appears to be part of the authentication by Jesus of the Gentile mission which took place later in the church. As the woman's perception of Jesus contrasts with the exclusive concerns of those closest to Jesus (with whom Mark's community would doubtless identify), Mark seems to be addressing both what may have been his church's claim to have an inside track on faithfulness and what may have been lingering concerns in that community about how to understand the Gentile presence.

Without the larger gospel context and the saying in verse 27, however, the Jewish-Gentile reference *within* Mark's version of this story is not clear. The picture underlying the exchange between Jesus and the woman is a simple one of a poor Palestinian household, in which family and pets shared the single room. In fact, the word translated "dogs" might better be translated as "puppies" or "house dogs." Thus one might hear Jesus' observation to mean, "Scarce bread needed for the children is not given to the family's pets." "But what the children drop," responds the woman, "the dogs will take." The logic is primarily that of the household and only secondarily that of salvation history.[8]

The Text Out of Context: The Questions Are Sharpened

To recognize that this story was elaborated in a way that brings into focus questions of Jewish-Gentile relations in the early church is still not to suggest that the story was composed by the church in order to address those concerns. To begin with, the earliest discernible form of the story need not be read as addressing Jewish-Gentile relations at all. Second, even if the saying in Mark's verse 27 is understood to be a proverb, and even if it was a metaphorical way of referring to the fact that the petitioner in this case is a Gentile, that saying addressed to the woman is offensive in the extreme. Metaphor or not, Jesus is depicted as comparing the woman and her daughter to dogs! No churchly or scholarly gymnastics are able to get around that problem. To note that the Greek word is a diminutive, meaning "puppies" or "little dogs," does not soften the saying, for, as Burkill points out, "As in English, so in other languages, to call a woman 'a little bitch' is no less abusive than to call her 'a bitch' without qualification."[9]

Jesus' flippant, even cruel, response to the woman defies justification. Try as we might, we really cannot see in this story a cozy domestic scene with family and pets happily coexisting under one roof and under the leadership of a benevolent householder (who becomes the stand-in for the Sovereign Christ in an inclusive church). We also do not find Jesus simply testing the woman's faith by an initially contrived and only apparent rejection.[10] Equally hard to recognize here is Taylor's claim to find in this story a glimpse of an incident in Jesus' life, but even more a glimpse into Jesus' psyche, showing that at this point in his life there was "tension in the mind of Jesus concerning the scope of his ministry." "He is speaking to Himself as well as to the woman," Taylor concludes (wishfully, I think). "Her reply shows that she is quick to perceive this."[11] Apparently (though Taylor does not draw this conclusion), it would then have been her tolerance of Jesus' indecision that allowed her to swallow the insult.

The shocking quality of the portrait of Jesus, plus the indications of internal development in the story, suggest to me that instead of composing this story to address contemporary church problems, the early church—at least from Mark's day on—made the best of a bizarre tradition about Jesus which it received. The very strangeness and the offensiveness of the story's portrayal of Jesus may suggest that the core of the story was indeed remembered as an incident in Jesus' life when even he was caught with his compassion down. I would suggest further that the story was originally remembered and retold in the community not for its ecclesiastical significance but primarily because of its christological significance. It tells us something about Jesus as the Christ, and only consequently something about us as the church.

In order to explore the christological significance of this story, and perhaps to hear afresh a word through the text to our own day, we will need to consider the account by itself, outside the framework that Mark provides. We will need to hear it as a story, a story-within-a-larger-story, drawing us into itself through its characters and their interaction. Obviously the leading character in the larger Gospel story is Jesus, but in this particular episode the protagonist is the Gentile woman.

On Gifts and Ministries: The Woman's Story

We know at once very little and a lot about her. She is a resident of the Gentile region including the cities of Tyre and Sidon. She was thus a foreigner to Jesus in an ethnic sense; she was a woman, and in fact a woman alone.[12] She may have been a widow, or divorced, or never married. In any event, she appears to be totally isolated from family support, for if there had been any male relative in her family (or among her in-laws if she had been married), he would have had the responsibility of caring for her and her daughter and of interceding on their behalf. Perhaps these family members, if there were any, lived at a great distance. Or perhaps for some reason they chose no longer to acknowledge the woman as part of their circle. She may have had sons somewhere, but if she were widowed or divorced they would probably have been taken over by her in-laws.

When we meet her, she is left with a daughter. In her society's terms that is a further liability, for daughters were not greatly valued. Sons were the focus of one's hopes and one's longing. Daughters usually cost money (at least for a dowry) and were often regarded as troublesome pieces of property weighing on their families until they could be safely married off to a suitable husband. In addition, we know that according to the customs of first-century Palestinian society, this woman should have been invisible. No Jewish man, especially one with a religious task or vocation, expected to be approached by a woman (Jew or Gentile), except perhaps by one of the many lone women reduced to prostitution to support themselves.

But we know some other things about the particular woman in this story. Apparently she did not accept the low esteem in which her society held her daughter, or its restrictions on her own behavior. She did not hesitate to approach Jesus, and even actively to importune him. And she valued her daughter, this one fundamentally like her who was still with her, who was suffering, and whose life was precious enough to demand healing and transformation, liberation from the alien forces that appeared to have taken her over. For the sake of her daughter, the woman broke custom, went after what she needed, and stood up to this visiting rabbi and miracle worker of whom so many stories had doubtless been told. And she bested him in an argument. Finally, she got what she wanted: Her daughter was healed.

Insofar as this is a story about a ministry, it is traditionally seen as an account of Jesus' healing ministry to this woman and her daughter. Hearing the story with ears tuned to women's experience, we might also point to the woman's intercessory ministry on behalf of her daughter. But there are two other dimensions of ministry suggested in both the Markan and Matthean accounts. First, there is the woman's ministry in a general sense as a witness to Jesus. In Mark her witness is primarily to him as miracle worker, but also to him as one whose attention and help could be won by persistence. Matthew helps us to recognize this witnessing ministry of the woman most clearly by the way he tells the story. We are led into the incident by the woman herself; we see it from her point of view. We are with her at the edge of the company around Jesus. We hear her words, and we hear and feel the response she gets. This greater use of direct discourse underlines the fact that this woman belongs in the company of others who by their active importuning (which is called by Matthew "faith," here and elsewhere) proclaim who Jesus is.

The second additional dimension of ministry present in the story is the woman's ministry *to* Jesus by her "faith"—a faith that is no doctrinal confession of his messianic identity, and no flattery of his apparently miraculous powers, but rather an act of trust, of engagement, risking everything. That act has the effect, as the story is told, of enabling Jesus to see the situation in a different way. That new perspective appears to free Jesus to respond, to heal, to become again the channel of God's redeeming presence in that situation. Whatever provoked the initial response attributed to Jesus (whether we should conclude that he was tired, or in a bad mood, or even that he appears to have participated in the racism and sexism that characterized his society), it is the Gentile woman who is said to have called his bluff. In so doing, she seems to have enabled him to act in a way apparently blocked to him before. Her wit, her sharp retort, was indeed her gift to Jesus—a gift that enabled his gift of healing in turn, her ministry that opened up the possibility of his. Her gift was not the submission or obedience seen as appropriate for women in her society, but rather the gift of sharp insight—the particular insight of the poor and outcast who can see through a situation because they have few illusions to defend. Her gift was also the gift of courage—the courage of those who have little more to lose and therefore can act in commitment and from faith on behalf of others, for the sake of life, wholeness, and liberation. Indeed, these highly political and encouraging words describe the quality of Jesus' ministry to this woman and to her daughter.

Thus, behind whatever ecclesiastical significance the church has found in this story, there appears to be a christological point: It sets forth who Jesus is as the Christ of God. The hallmarks of that identity, here as elsewhere in the gospel tradition, are qualities and actions of life and freedom, made known in painful human interaction. Elsewhere those who see themselves as the privileged people in social or religious terms are shown struggling to comprehend this Christ who so often offends them, while the "poor"—the economically poor and socially outcast, the sick, the oppressed, the rejected —respond joyfully to the good news of God's reign. Here Jesus himself must learn about being that sort of Christ from one of the poorest of the poor and most despised of the outcast—a Gentile woman on her own before God and humankind. Her gifts and her ministry become the vehicle of the gospel to Jesus and to us. And we who hear and tell her story say, "So be it."

6

"Mother in Israel": A Familiar Figure Reconsidered[1]

J. Cheryl Exum

After a great military victory led by a woman, jubilation gives rise to a song, which celebrates the exciting events and captures them for posterity.

> In the days of Shamgar, son of Anath,
>   in the days of Jael, caravans ceased
>   and travelers kept to the byways.
> The peasantry ceased in Israel, they ceased
>   until you arose, Deborah,
>   arose as a mother in Israel.
> (Judges 5:6–7)[2]

What does it mean to call Deborah, of whom we do not know that she had children, a "mother in Israel"? Commentators, if they treat this part of the verse at all, are not in agreement. I want to use the concept "mother in Israel" as both my starting and end point to examine a familiar role, one that so often defines and determines the meaning of a woman's life in biblical times, at least according to (mostly male) biblical scholars. First, however, a word about my method and intention.

I do not wish to defend the Bible or deny its patriarchal bias. Like the wider theological enterprise, both the Bible and the history of biblical scholarship stand in need of feminist critique. Scholars have begun to examine the biblical material from a nonandrocentric perspective, and much remains to be done.[3] A variety of methods should aid us in this task. Sociological and anthropological studies shed light on women's status in biblical times.[4] Literary approaches reveal attitudes toward women and reflect a variety of opinions about their contributions, real or idealized, to the community of faith. My approach here involves primarily a literary method of close reading, which pays careful attention to the portrayal of women in selected texts. Within the admittedly patriarchal context of the biblical literature, we find strong countercurrents of affirmation of women: stories that show women's courage, strength, faith, ingenuity, talents, dignity, and worth. Such stories undermine patriarchal assumptions and temper patriarchal biases, often challenging the very patriarchal structures that dominate the narrative landscape [57].

In the interest of space, I have chosen to look at the figure of mother, not only because motherhood so often defines "woman's place" but frankly also because mothers are not to me the most interesting among the large cast of women in the Bible. I have chosen the figure in part, then, because of her ordinariness— mothers are not major characters. With the exception of Deborah, the women to be discussed here derive their significance from the fact that they gave birth to famous sons. But close examination reveals that these mothers are not so ordinary after all, and their influence is far-reaching. A striking paradox emerges in these stories of mothers: Whereas the important events in Israelite tradition are experienced by men, they are often set in motion and determined by women. This is especially clear in the matriarchal stories of Genesis 12—36, where the famous sons represent Israel personified and their mothers are responsible for Israel's becoming what it becomes. Since space demands even further selectivity, not all biblical mothers, or even all the more important ones, can be considered[5]; rather, I have selected a few, some well-known, some obscure to the point of being nameless. These examples come from three important biblical periods: the patriarchal and matriarchal period, the beginnings of the exodus, and the period of the judges. I hope that my necessarily limited comments upon them will be suggestive of what could and should be done on a larger scale. Unfortunately we cannot continue into the period of the monarchy, where the same patterns and paradox prevail (the classic example is Bathsheba), nor beyond into the exile and restoration to explore the disruption of the pattern, and ultimately into New Testament times, where the familiar themes are reappropriated (Luke 1:5–25) and reshaped (Matt. 1:18–25; Luke 1:26–56). Also, by starting with the matriarchs, we pass over the existentially most important woman and one of the most fascinating figures, Eve, "mother of all living," source of the human condition as we know it.[6]

The Mothers of All Israel

The stories of the patriarchs and matriarchs in Genesis 12—50 are stories about a promise, the threefold promise to Abraham of numerous descendants, the land of Canaan, and the role as mediator of God's blessing to all humanity—a promise passed from Abraham to his son, to his son, and so on down the male line. Numerous obstacles threaten the promise, postponing its fulfillment: for example, the barrenness (11:30; 16:1; 29:31) or potential loss (chs. 12; 20; 26) of the matriarch; the fact that the patriarch and his wife are too old to bear children (17:17; 18:12); or the command to Abraham to sacrifice his son, "your only son Isaac, whom you love" (Gen. 22:2; never mind that Abraham has another son, Ishmael). Every listener to these stories knows the outcome in advance, for the patriarchs are personifications of the collective memory of Israel, and the hearers are the heirs to the promise. The delight is in the telling. In the figures of the patriarchs, Israel sees itself and its special relationship to God, and in these stories Israel reveals itself, holding up for our scrutiny both positive and negative aspects of its character.

What, then, is the role of the matriarchs? Obviously, to bear the children of the promise—thus the importance of the "right" wife: Sarah, not Hagar, must be the mother of the rightful heir; Isaac and Jacob may not have Canaanite—that is, "foreign"—wives (24:3; 27:46; 28:1). Not only must the "right" woman be the mother of the chosen people, the "right" son must be the bearer of the promise (Isaac and not Ishmael, Jacob and not Esau). In the patriarchal world, males are the significant figures: Abraham follows the divine call to the promised land; Sarah is "taken" with him (notice how Sarah is objectified and repeatedly " taken" in Genesis 12). Women are simply ignored in numerous scenes: the Genesis narrators are interested in Abraham's faith, not Sarah's (Genesis 22); Jacob wrestles with God in "face to face" combat (Gen. 32:30), while Rachel's "mighty wrestlings" are with her sister (Gen. 30:8). Typically, the matriarchs are omitted from recitals of faith (Deut. 26:5; Josh. 24: 2–13; 1 Sam. 12:8–11; Psalm 105—notice what this psalm does with Genesis 12 and 20; but cf. Isa. 51:2). On the other hand, when the matriarchs appear as actors, they come to life as fully developed personalities, whose struggles and determination are deftly sketched and whose joys and sorrows become real for us. In such stories, they are not appendages of the patriarchs but rather persons in their own right—women participating in a patriarchal culture but sometimes pictured as standing over against it. This is our paradox: Though frequently ignored in the larger story of Israel's journey toward the promise, the matriarchs act at strategic points that move the plot, and thus the promise, in the proper direction toward its fulfillment. We must confine our attention to the most important examples, though for a full appreciation of the matriarchs and their contributions, all the stories that deal with them, as well as those that ignore them, need to be considered [133].

The major events in the lives of the matriarchs center around their sons. The barren matriarch is a common theme, since barrenness provides a threat that the needed son might not appear and offers an opportunity for the deity to intervene (cf. also Judges 13, discussed below, and 1 Samuel 1). In Genesis 16, Sarah speaks for the first time and thus for the first time comes to life as a character. She initiates the action and controls it throughout the six verses in which she appears. In contrast to what has gone before, Abraham is the passive figure here: he obeys Sarah (RSV, "hearkened to the voice of" Sarah, v. 2) and acknowledges her authority over the situation ("your maid is in your power," v. 6). For the first time we see things from Sarah's point of view.[7] This, however, presents a rather complex situation because the narrator of our tale is our source for Sarah's point of view, and the narrative point of view is androcentric, uncritical of patriarchy.

To be childless in a patriarchal society represents a loss of status. Sarah, who recognizes the ultimate responsibility of the deity, is the first to offer a concrete solution to the major obstacle to the promise, the absence of an heir. She gives her Egyptian maid Hagar to Abraham, not simply so that Abraham might have an heir (he could take another wife to bear him children but does not; he takes another wife only after Sarah is dead, 25:1), but rather because, according to this custom, Hagar's child would be considered Sarah's. That this particular means of obtaining children is for the woman's sake and not the man's is also clear from Genesis 29—30, where Rachel and Leah give their maids to Jacob even though he already has sons. Sarah's plan backfires, however, when the pregnant Hagar becomes arrogant, thus presenting a different kind of challenge to Sarah's status, her superior status as primary wife. Again, Sarah must act, this time to guarantee her position. She treats Hagar harshly, and Hagar flees (another threat to the promise, that Hagar the Egyptian might become the mother of Israel, is thus thwarted). God, however, in one of the few theophanies to a woman, instructs Hagar to return and submit to Sarah (which poses the threat anew).

The story gives us poignant insight into the plight of both Sarah and Hagar. Hagar in particular deserves to be approached from a

feminist perspective, which views her as a paradigm of the oppressed woman who has the courage to seek freedom (an odd reversal of the exodus paradigm, for here an Egyptian flees oppression
by Israel). She becomes the mother of a great nation characterized
by its refusal to be submissive.[8] Yet although the story is told with
sympathy for Sarah and sensitivity toward Hagar, a feminist critique
recognizes its painful limitations. Both Sarah and Hagar are victims
of a patriarchal society that stresses the importance of sons and of
a narrative structure that revolves around the promise of a son.
Sadly, but not surprisingly in such a context, they make victims of
each other. The story describes the privileged woman's exploitation
of her subordinate. Sarah uses Hagar (how Hagar feels about being
given to Abraham as a wife is not stated), and Hagar apparently
covets Sarah's position (the oppressed seeking to change places
with the oppressor), so that Sarah must oppress Hagar in order to
assert herself. It is a vicious circle in which women are played off
against each other in the quest for status, a situation we shall see
reflected in the conflict between Rachel and Leah. When a critical
feminist perspective is brought to bear upon the narrative, Sarah's
anger at Abraham, "May the Lord judge between you and me" (not
"between Hagar and me"; Gen. 16:5), becomes an indictment of the
patriarchal system, which pits women against women and challenges their intrinsic worth with patriarchal presuppositions about
women's role [55, 56].

Genesis 17 and 18 give increasing attention to Sarah ("I will bless
her, and she shall be a mother of nations," 17:16) and the promised
birth of her son. Finally Sarah bears the long-awaited heir. Genesis
21 resolves once and for all the threat posed to the promise by the
presence of Hagar and Ishmael. Earlier, Sarah had acted to secure
her own position; now she moves to protect Isaac's inheritance by
having Hagar and Ishmael sent away. Though Abraham is dis-
pleased, Sarah's position receives divine approval (the threat must
be removed, and God here works through Sarah to remove it):
"Whatever Sarah says to you, do as she tells you, for through Isaac
shall your descendants be named" (21:12; cf. 25:6, where Abraham
expels his other sons). On a feminist reading, both women suffer:
One is cast out, becoming the mother of a great nation excluded
from the covenant; the other stays within the patriarchal hearth and
almost loses her only child to the father. Sarah does not appear in
the story of the near sacrifice of Isaac in Genesis 22. It is, after all,
a test of Abraham, just as Genesis 12:1–3 was the call of Abraham.
On Abraham's faith, not Sarah's, hangs the whole divine experi-
ment. Sarah's death, recorded in Genesis 23:2, receives elaboration
in a later midrash, which relates that she dropped dead upon hear-

ing what Abraham was prepared to do (Tanhuma, Par. Uayira 23).

Isaac is comforted after his mother's death by his marriage to Rebekah (Gen. 24:67), a brief but touching testimony to the bond between mother and son. We must skip the wonderful introduction to Rebekah in Genesis 24, where she reveals her generosity and initiative, in order to focus on her pivotal role in obtaining for Jacob the patriarchal blessing. Like Sarah, Rebekah is at first barren; but when Isaac offers an intercessory prayer, she conceives twins (Gen. 25:21–24). The struggle between Jacob and Esau begins even before their birth, and the anxious mother-to-be seeks a divine oracle (without benefit of either patriarchal or priestly intercession). She receives an answer to which she alone is privy: "The elder shall serve the younger" (Gen. 25:23). Thus Rebekah knows from the outset—as we know and as the ancient listeners knew—how things will turn out. And thus she loves Jacob (Gen. 25:28).

Is it coincidence that Rebekah is listening when Isaac reveals his intention to bless Esau (Gen. 27:1–5)? Immediately she sets her plan into motion; her favorite son has only to follow her instructions ("Obey my word," vs. 8, 13). But Jacob fears that discovery of the ruse by his father might bring him a curse rather than a blessing, an understandable reluctance given the seriousness of the curse, which, once uttered, proceeds immutable toward its realization. Rebekah's response, "Upon me be your curse, my son," demonstrates her remarkable resolve. What has Jacob to lose? It is Rebekah who risks everything. She prepares the food that Isaac loves so that Jacob can present it to him. She dresses Jacob in Esau's clothes and outfits him with animal skins so that he will both smell and feel like his older brother and thereby deceive his blind father. With all the details taken care of by his mother, Jacob proceeds to carry out the ruse and succeeds in getting for himself the coveted blessing— only moments before his brother returns, ready to claim what is rightfully his. Clearly, Jacob owes his success to the timely and decisive action of his strong-willed and resourceful mother.

Justifiably angry, Esau determines to kill Jacob. Rebekah (typically well informed) learns of the plan and again acts decisively, this time to preserve Jacob's life. Again she gives him all-important instructions ("Obey my voice," v. 43): Jacob must flee to her brother Laban until Esau's anger has subsided and she sends for him. She even manages (27:46—28:5) to get Isaac to send him away, with a blessing, to take a wife from Rebekah's family. Israel (Jacob) sets out on its journey toward fulfillment of its destiny, on a course charted by his mother.

Jacob acquires two wives, and he loves one more than the other (Gen. 29:30). This situation gives rise to a variation of the barrenness motif: only the favored wife is initially barren; God blesses the other with fertility, a compensation for being unloved by her husband. Genesis 29—30 describes a child-bearing contest between the rival sisters through which Israel is built up (the twelve sons of Jacob represent the twelve tribes of Israel, and the promise of numerous descendants is on its way toward fulfillment). We are again aware of the androcentric perspective, which values a woman for her ability to produce sons (the daughter Dinah receives only passing mention, 30:21).

Leah believes that by mothering Jacob's firstborn son she will gain the patriarch's affection: "Surely now my husband will love me" (29:32). In quick succession she bears three more sons. Rachel envies her sister's fruitfulness and vents her frustration on Jacob (30:1). Like Sarah's anger at Abraham (16:5), the woman's dissatisfaction with her position receives recognition, but the real source of the problem, the patriarchal system, remains unrecognized, and the matriarchs can only aim their frustration at the patriarchs. Both women now give their maid to Jacob in order to obtain children, and Bilhah and Zilpah each bear two sons. Whereas the narrative encourages us to feel sympathy for Leah, who is not loved, and for Rachel, who longs for a child but has none, it also invites us to laugh. While there is something ludicrous in the preoccupation with producing sons, the real butt of our laughter is none other than the patriarch himself, whose sexual services are traded for some aphrodisiacs. Imagine Jacob coming in from a day's work in the fields to be met by his triumphant unloved wife with the words, "You must come in to me, for I have hired you with my son's mandrakes" (30:16). Is this any way to treat the great patriarch of Israel? Not unexpectedly, Leah bears another son and, later, a sixth. She seems to have given up her expectation of winning Jacob's love (29:32) for the more modest goal of gaining his respect, "Now my husband will honor me, because I have borne him six sons" (30:20).

When at last (Gen. 30:22) "God remembered Rachel" and "hearkened to her and opened her womb," the contest between the sisters comes to an end. But this occurs only after Rachel took the initiative to solve the problem of barrenness with the mandrakes (perhaps they were effective?). Eleven of the twelve tribes are now accounted for. Later in the Genesis narrative, Rachel will bear the twelfth. But because she dies in childbirth, this last son is not the source of joy (see Gen. 35:16–20).

This rapid survey has centered on a recurrent theme in the matriarchal stories: Because of its mothers, Israel becomes a people numerous and blessed. Sarah guarantees Isaac's inheritance against the threat of Ishmael. Rebekah sees to it that Jacob obtains the blessing. And Rachel and Leah, in their competition to provide Jacob with sons, build up the house of Israel. At the same time, reviewing these stories makes us aware of the limitations placed upon the matriarchs by the patriarchal system that the Bible takes for granted. Bearing sons is of utmost importance, and the matriarchs' major accomplishments are for the sake of their sons. Israel is personified in its sons, not its mothers.

The Mothers of the Exodus

Here we shall concentrate on the mothers of Moses, not only his natural mother but also his adoptive mother, the daughter of Pharaoh, and the contribution they make to the exodus event. They are mothers of the exodus because of the role they play as mothers of its great leader, Moses. But as we consider their story, we should keep in mind that the exodus has three figurative mothers as well: Shiphrah and Puah, the midwives who defy Pharaoh's command to kill male Hebrew babies, and Moses' sister, whose resourcefulness at a strategic moment determines Moses' future and who later becomes a leader of the exodus in her own right. The liberation of Israel from bondage in Egypt begins in the courageous actions— and disobedience—of women. It begins when women refuse to cooperate with oppression, relying on wisdom to foil the designs of a foolish Pharaoh and thereby bringing life out of threatened death.

In Exodus 2, two daughters determine the course of history, the daughter of Levi (as Moses' mother is called in v. 1) and the daughter of Pharaoh. Their actions are subversive. Whereas the disobedience of the two midwives takes the form of noncompliance (they act by choosing not to act in accordance with Pharaoh's edict), Moses' mother and Pharaoh's daughter openly disobey Pharaoh's command to expose male infants in the Nile (Ex. 1:22).[9] Pharaoh's daughter, as the counterfoil to her oppressive father, does, in fact, precisely the opposite: She takes the baby out of the Nile!

Though Moses' mother does not speak at all in the narrative, her actions display more than words could tell us of her concern to save her child. First she hides him. When that is no longer possible, she takes elaborate care to prepare a little ark (RSV, "basket") for her son in which to set him afloat on the Nile (note the ironic contrast: Pharaoh wanted the baby in the Nile, but not like this!). The only other ark in the Bible is Noah's, and the connection between Noah and Moses as saviors who are saved from drowning is inescapable. Whereas Noah builds the ark that saves humanity from destruction, Moses' mother builds the ark that, by saving its future leader, enables the delivery of Israel from bondage. Much activity is attributed to her in Exodus 2:2–3: She does not simply wait for some miracle to save her son; rather, one might say, she sets the stage for something miraculous to happen. All, apparently, without counsel or assistance from her husband.

As if by design, Pharaoh's daughter comes to bathe in the Nile and spots the ark. When she discovers the crying infant inside, she has compassion (RSV, "took pity on him"). Significantly, we know the motivation of the women in this story: that of Moses' mother and sister to save their own flesh and blood is self-evident; the midwives act out of desire to live according to the will of God (the meaning of "fear of God"), and Pharaoh's daughter is moved by compassion, an emotion that extends beyond ethic boundaries. She recognizes the child as Hebrew (2:6) and in violation of her father's edict saves him from the Nile. Prompted by the sister's clever, timely suggestion ("Shall I go and call you a nurse from the Hebrew women to nurse the child for you?"), she not only determines to keep the infant but even hires a Hebrew woman to nurse him. There is wonderful irony in the fact that Moses' mother is paid to nurse her own child. Paying wages is the princess's idea and may be her way of attesting the right of possession to the child.[10] Thus she accentuates what Moses' sister had only intimated; she claims the child as her own, offering protection in the house of the oppressor to the future liberator of his people (another delicious irony). At the end of the story, he becomes her son and she names him Moshe, "the drawer out," a name that augurs his future role as leader of the exodus.

Though she gives a name, Pharaoh's daughter has none. Nor are other characters identified in this story, with the exception of Moses, Shiphrah, and Puah (the magnitude of the midwives' deed, comparable in its own way to Moses' deliverance of the people, demands that we not forget their names). Moses' mother is later identified as Jochebed (Ex. 6:20; Num. 26:59). While she and Pharaoh's daughter do not participate in subsequent events (nor does Moses' father, incidentally), Moses' sister takes on a major role in the exodus.

The similarities between Moses' mothers and the matriarchs are readily apparent. The action of mothers determines the future for Israel, but it is a future lived out primarily by sons. Women have a significant role in Exodus 1:15—2:10, but the goal of the story is the birth of a son who will become the great leader of his people. Though his life will again be saved by a woman (Ex. 4:24–26), Moses will soon take over center stage, even to the point of overshadowing God in the exodus narrative. Our paradox remains: Without Moses there would be no exodus, but without these women there would be no Moses!

I have dealt at length in another study[11] with the women in the prologue to the exodus, which in part justifies my brevity here. I must confess that I was never satisfied with the results. The reason, I believe, has to do with disappointment that the narrative quickly and thoroughly moves from a woman's story to a man's story. While a feminist critique might want to seize onto the affirmative dimension of our paradox, accenting the important consequences of women's actions for the divine plan, it must also acknowledge that being mothers of heroes—albeit daring, enterprising, and tenacious mothers—is not enough; acting behind the scenes is not enough. The exception in the exodus story is Moses' sister, later identified as Miriam, whom I have not discussed here because she is not a mother. In addition to her leadership role in the exodus (see, for example, Numbers 12, where she commands enough authority to challenge Moses, and Micah 6:4, which places her on an equal footing with Moses and Aaron), she shares with Deborah (see below) the designation as prophet and the attribution of a famous victory song (Exodus 15). She deserves, in addition to our admiration, greater critical attention.

Two Mothers from the Period of the Judges

The mother of Samson (Judges 13) differs from the mothers considered thus far in that she does not do anything to affect either her son's or Israel's destiny. In a sense, she is the most "ordinary" mother, and yet her story is a wonderful one, which affirms her as a person and as a mother. It does so in two ways: by refusing to let her husband steal the limelight in spite of all his efforts, and by attributing to her a goodly share of theological insight.[12] Her story is also unusual. Although she has the central role, her husband is named while she is not. Like other famous mothers, she is at first barren, but there are no indications that she regards her situation as critical. We are not told that she is old, as was Sarah, nor does she complain about childlessness, as does Rachel (Gen. 30:1). She does not pray for a son, as does Hannah (1 Sam. 1:11), nor does her husband pray for her as Isaac prayed for Rebekah. Nor does she take extraordinary measures to obtain children, like Sarah, Rachel, and Leah, who gave their maids to their husbands, or like Rachel, who used aphrodisiacs.

The woman alone is the recipient of a theophany in which she learns she will bear a son and receives instructions about him (Judg. 13:3–5). Her husband, Manoah, knows only what she tells him about this event, and, interestingly, she leaves out some important information (that their son may not be shaved and that he will begin to deliver Israel from the Philistines). The essentials, however, what she must do and the boy's destiny as a Nazirite, are all there.

Manoah's prayer that the man "come again to us, and teach us what we are to do with the boy that will be born" (v. 8) is odd, since his wife has already informed him. In my opinion, what Manoah is really asking for here is to be included in an encounter with the man in which he, too, receives special information. Notice, however, that though Manoah's prayer is granted, it does not happen in the way Manoah has requested. The messenger appears (v. 9) not "to us" but again to the woman alone, a point underscored by the words "but Manoah her husband was not with her." Rather than having the messenger appear to him, Manoah must be brought to the messenger by his wife (posing for us the question whether Manoah would ever have seen the messenger were it not for the woman's intervention). Finally, Manoah gets the audience he wants, but— unlike his wife, who behaves with the proper reserve before such an honored emissary (v. 6)—he is brimming with questions. Ironically, however, for all his efforts, he receives even less information from the messenger than he had received from his wife. The messenger merely turns the issue back to the woman: "Of all that I said to the woman let her beware" (v. 13). By denying Manoah as much knowledge about the child as his wife, the narrative stresses her importance. It also portrays her as more perceptive than Manoah.

Together Manoah and his wife prepare an offering, which provides the occasion for the messenger's divine identity to be revealed. Up to this point, the couple have referred to him as a "man of God," a title sometimes used for a prophet. The text singles out Manoah's lack of perception ("For Manoah did not know that he was the angel of the Lord," v. 16), followed by his recognition of the messenger's identity (v. 21). Nothing is said about the woman's not knowing the messenger's divine status. On the contrary, she sensed it from the start, "His countenance was like the countenance of the angel of God—very terrible" (v. 6). The response of husband and wife to the revelation further reflects their different comprehension of the situation. Good theologian that he is, Manoah realizes that one cannot see God and live (cf. Ex. 33:20; Judg. 6:22–23; Gen. 16:13–14; Ex. 19:21; Gen. 32:30). His wife, however, is a better theologian, for she recognizes the divine purpose behind the events and is therefore able to assure her husband that they will not die (in theophanies, it is usually the deity who gives this assurance). This lovely story puts Manoah in his place; he neither knows as much about his child's destiny nor understands the divine intention as well as his wife. To its patriarchal society, to Manoah, and to us, it teaches that the figure of the mother and her importance may not be overshadowed by the father.

From an obscure mother, we turn to the most famous woman of the period and one of the few examples of a strong, independent woman in the Bible. Deborah boasts an extraordinary number of accomplishments. Although the exact duties of the judges are not clear, some appear to have exercised legal and administrative functions while others were charismatic military leaders. Deborah combines these two important offices in addition to holding a third one, that of prophet. People came to her for judgment, which suggests she was well known for her legal decisions (Judg. 4:5). She also led an Israelite coalition to victory in a strategic battle against the militarily superior Canaanites (see Judges 4 and 5). A review of the book of Judges reveals Deborah as one of the few unsullied leaders. She is followed by a series of male judges who display unexpected weaknesses and serious faults (Gideon, Jephthah, Samson).

Deborah's general is Barak, and not a few commentators accentuate his role while playing down hers. Some call him a judge (the text does not) and point out that Barak leads the troops, while Deborah merely summons him.[13] Deborah's function, however, might be compared with that of another judge and prophet, Samuel, who anoints Saul king and sends him off to fight the Lord's battles (see esp. 1 Sam. 10—15). Deborah commissions Barak. In her capacity as prophet, she summons him with a message from the Lord, sending him into battle with a promise of victory. Barak appears accountable to Deborah in the way that Samuel holds Saul accountable to him (and the Lord). Some interesting similarities also exist between Deborah and the Canaanite goddess of war, Anat, who has a subordinate to carry out her commands.[14] It is important to note that Barak refuses to go into battle unless Deborah accompanies him, which she does (Judg. 4:9, 10). Moreover, Deborah prophesies that the victory will not bring glory to Barak but rather to a woman (4:9). That woman, we discover later on, is not Deborah but another courageous woman, Jael.[15]

By virtue of the song attributed to her in Judges 5, Deborah may also be considered a singer of tales and a skilled poet. In 5:12 she is called to sing; 5:1 tells us she sang the song.[16] Whatever the song's origin, Deborah is remembered as its source and inspiration, and appropriately it is known by the title "The Song of Deborah." An acknowledged literary masterpiece, the poem, in addition to praising Deborah and describing the battle, devotes considerable attention to two other women, Jael and Sisera's mother, placed in striking juxtaposition at the conclusion.

Judges 4:4 identifies Deborah as an *'esheth lappidoth*, a phrase usually rendered "wife of Lappidoth" but which may be translated "fiery woman" (cf. the NEB footnote, "spirited woman"), a description that fits her admirably. If Lappidoth was her husband, it is interesting to note that the narrative has nothing else to say about him. Though we cannot be sure the text calls her a wife, it does call her a mother, and thus we return to the question raised at the beginning of this chapter: What does it mean to call Deborah a mother in Israel? Her accomplishments described in Judges 4—5 include counsel, inspiration, and leadership.[17] A mother in Israel is one who brings liberation from oppression, provides protection, and ensures the well-being and security of her people.[18]

Even though she is not a biological mother like the others, I have included Deborah in this brief look at mothers because her presence as a leader and hero among a biblical cast of mostly male leaders and heroes calls attention by contrast to the more usual position of women bound by patriarchal strictures. Yet the other women we have looked at, while acting behind the scenes in more traditional roles, emerge as important characters. In the sense that they too ensure the welfare and fortune of their people, the patriarchs and the mothers of the exodus are also "mothers in Israel." Our paradox, that women often play crucial roles but are rarely major characters, calls for a bifocal approach to the biblical material: on the one hand, to appreciate the contributions of women which the Bible records, and on the other hand, and at the same time, to be critical of the Bible's androcentric perspective. Such an approach enables us to read the stories of a Deborah or a Miriam as a critique of a patriarchal culture that produced too few independent female leaders, and it allows us to praise the strengths of those women who appear in stereotyped, subordinate roles.

7

Prophets and Pornography: Female Sexual Imagery in Hosea

T. Drorah Setel

For women living in Western cultures deeply influenced by Jewish and Christian traditions, the Hebrew Bible is a central document in a historical exploration of patriarchy.[1] It is a compilation of materials that span approximately one thousand years of human experience. Even if it is taken primarily as a literary rather than a historically accurate text, the Hebrew Bible (like *all* ancient Near Eastern material) provides information concerning an extensive period in the formation of patriarchal societies. It therefore deserves serious attention as evidence of the historical bases of contemporary institutions and perspectives, while modern feminist thought can, in turn, serve to illuminate and redefine biblical interpretation [55].

One example of a significant aspect of patriarchy that may be better understood through the interaction between biblical material and feminist theory is the objectification of female sexuality. Although feminist discussion has focused extensively on the nature and effects of objectification in the form of contemporary pornography, examination of biblical texts shows an interesting congruence between ancient and modern depictions of female sexuality. This is particularly evident in the writings that comprise the second part of the division of Prophets in the Hebrew Bible: the books of Isaiah, Jeremiah, Ezekiel, and the twelve "shorter" prophets. While these writings reflect views of female sexuality current in the history of the Israelites before that time, they appear to develop a specific use of female imagery that does not occur in previous periods. They seem to be the first to use objectified female sexuality as a symbol of evil.

In an attempt to understand the emergence of this imagery in prophetic writings, it is important to examine (1) contemporary theory on the nature of female objectification, (2) the historical development of biblical views of female sexuality prior to the prophetic writings, and (3) the prophetic material in light of those theoretical and historical frameworks. It is, of course, beyond the scope of this presentation to discuss each area in detail. I will therefore focus on the last—that is to say, an analysis of prophetic literature—after a brief summary of its theoretical and historical setting.

The Nature of Female Objectification

The primary relationship between a dualistic worldview and the objectification of women has been a key tenet of feminist theory for more than thirty years.[2] More recently, feminists have begun to explore in greater detail the nature of that objectification specifically as it relates to female sexuality. Most of this study, though not all, has taken place within the context of an attempt to analyze the nature and implications of pornography. In the course of this work, there has emerged an understanding of pornography as both a description of and a tool for maintaining male domination of female sexuality.

In summarizing the theoretical material on pornography so as to apply it to historical inquiry, we are able to distinguish four categories of analysis: features, function, definitions, and causes.[3]

The distinguishing *features* of pornography can be characterized as follows: (1) Female sexuality is depicted as negative in relationship to a positive and neutral male standard; (2) women are degraded and publicly humiliated; and (3) female sexuality is portrayed as an object of male possession and control, which includes the depiction of women as analogous to nature in general and the land in particular, especially with regard to imagery of conquest and domination.

The *function* of pornography can be summarized as a maintenance of male domination through the denial, or misnaming, of female experience. Four general ways in which this denial occurs are: (1) the representation of female objectification as universal truth, rather than as an oppressive socially constructed reality that allows the tolerance and acceptance of female objectification as a normal and inevitable feature of human experience,[4] (2) a concern with *sex* and *men* rather than *male domination* and *women* as the "what" and "who" of pornography,[5] (3) teaching and/or expecting women to identify with a male perspective,[6] and (4) a failure to distinguish and, hence, a denial of the difference among the terms "prostitute" (as a nonjudgmental term to describe women who use their sexuality for economic subsistence), "harlot" (implying a woman whose sexuality is "not subject to control"), and "whore" (the object of male control and degradation).[7]

Feminist study has produced various *definitions* of pornography, which may be seen as complementary summaries of its nature. All the authors of the works I have consulted have included objectification as a fundamental criterion in addition, or relation, to defining pornography as: (1) "a statement about the restriction of fundamental choices for women," i.e., "slavery"[8]; (2) "material that explicitly represents or describes degrading and abusive sexual behavior so as to endorse and/or recommend the behavior as described," involving a distinction between pornography and "moral realism," an approach that condemns the behavior represented[9]; or (3) concerning "male power, its nature, its magnitude, its use, its meaning," and "the graphic depiction of women as vile whores."[10]

The *causes* of pornography suggested by feminist analysis are not its origins (which are assumed to be identical to the origins of objectification itself) but rather the bases of its growth. Two related perceptions develop out of the understanding that pornography asserts male domination. One is that pornography arises out of a psychological need for a sense of power and superiority as a proof of manhood.[11] A corollary to this may be the denial of individual or group powerlessness. The other cause posited by feminist theory is that pornography is the specific response to changes in the power relationship between women and men which may increase the autonomy of women.[12]

Biblical Views of Female Sexuality

Before going on to relate these perceptions and considerations of the nature of female objectification to its specific use in prophetic writing, we should consider briefly the historical background to prophetic views of female sexuality. These views may be categorized by three areas of emphasis: procreation, ritual purity, and possession.

In general terms, a preoccupation with the reproductive capabilities of women characterized the early history of the Israelites. Recent scholarship has begun to illuminate the relationship between the political and demographic concerns of the Israelites during the period of national formation in Canaan and their emphasis on the reproductive nature of women.[13]

Concurrent with the centralization of political power in the development of the monarchy was the expansion of an exclusively male priesthood. An important element of Israelite priestly power was the complicated ritual and ideological system of *tum'ah* and *taharah*, terms usually translated as "uncleanliness" and "cleanliness," although in this context it is more accurate to describe them as "taboo" *(tame)* and "ritually pure" *(tahor)* states of being.[14] The significance of this system for female sexuality is complex. Throughout the Hebrew Bible it is clear that the power of life and death is God's power. The fact that women are rendered "taboo" through the life-bearing functions of the reproductive cycle can be seen as a recognition of their participation in divine power.[15] At the same time, the system of ritual purity, by emphasizing the continual need to distinguish the realm of the divine from the realm of the human, serves to diminish—or even negate—the power of female human beings in the life process.[16] It may be seen as a means of male (priestly) control over what may have originally been perceived as female power on both a material (reproductive) and spiritual (pro-creative) level.

In this period the locus of female sexual activity is significant only inasmuch as it affects paternity [75]. Marriage is a property relationship; the terms usually translated as "wife" and "husband" are actually "woman" *(ishah)* and "master" *(ba'al)*. There is no verb "to marry"; a man "takes" a woman for himself, thus transferring her possession from her father's household to his own. Virginity is not an ethical but an economic condition; women who are sexually active while in their father's household diminish their property value in a marriage transaction.[17]

Descriptions of female sexual activity outside of marriage take two forms. One is adultery, which is a sexual relationship between a married woman and any man who is not her husband. Adultery is punishable by death. Again, this is a property valuation and not an ethical issue; it is paternity, not a woman's integrity, that is violated in an adulterous relationship.

The second category of nonmarital female sexual activity is *zenut,* which may be translated as "prostitution" or "harlotry." Prepro-phetic understanding of the term had two basic implications. One was an association with native Canaanite religion, which supposedly entailed ritualized sexual activity in which human sexuality was viewed as the embodiment of divine creative power. The other meaning of *zenut* is as a description of the nonreligious activity and status of women. Although, in this context, *zonah* certainly indicates "prostitute," it is without any inherently pejorative connotation. The role of prostitutes in the structure of Israelite society has yet to be adequately researched, but it has been suggested that they constituted an established urban group outside of the unity of family and household and, by implication, the system of marriage and female control.[18] Within the framework of a concern for paternity, it is certainly imaginable that there existed a toleration, if not encouragement, of the sexual availability of women who, whether by choice or circumstance, were not under the control of a husband or father.

Thus, in the centuries before the prophetic writings, female sexuality was at first viewed primarily as the power to give birth. This power was then constricted by placing the status of motherhood within the confines of the system of ritual purity. In addition, the worth of women's procreative capabilities became a property valuation transferred from father to husband. Female sexual activity that diminished the property value of a woman's body was discouraged; that which challenged the paternity of a husband was strongly prohibited. Sexual activity that did not disrupt the paternity system was tolerated.

Bound up with these developments was the growth of a perspective that sought to distinguish and separate, rather than integrate, categories of experience. Examination of prophetic writings with regard to an understanding of their use of female sexual imagery implies not only a specific concern with that imagery itself but also a consideration of the extent to which it is a manifestation of this larger patriarchal perspective.

Female Sexual Imagery in Hosea

The rest of this discussion will focus on the writings of the eighth-century B.C.E. prophet Hosea, in which female sexual imagery plays a central thematic role. A primary means by which the prophet conveys his perception of the relationship between Israel and God is through the metaphor of his own marriage. In the course of representing those relationships, Hosea makes extensive use of terms and imagery related to sexuality. Some of these depictions are significant in other prophetic writings as well, while some of them appear to be unique to Hosea.

The second verse of Hosea introduces the central theme of the first three chapters of the book:

> When Yahweh first spoke with Hosea,
> Yahweh said to Hosea:
>> "Go, take yourself a wife of harlotry,
>> and have children of harlotry,
>> for the land commits great harlotry
>> by departing from Yahweh."
>>> (Hosea 1:2)[19]

The words translated here as "harlotry" are all from the same root as the words *zenut* and *zonah*. As discussed earlier, these terms are used descriptively in reference to prostitution, as well as in the evaluative context of depicting Canaanite religious practice.

A third aspect of *zenut,* implied by this passage and others in Hosea, is "harlotry" in the specific sense of "not subject to control." In their commentary on Hosea, F. I. Andersen and D. N. Freedman point out that the book never uses the descriptive term *zonah* (i.e., "prostitute") but uses, instead, the term *zenunim* and the verb *zanah,* which they translate as "promiscuity" and "to be promiscuous," respectively.[20] In a context of specific concern with female imagery, however, "harlot" and "harlotry" are more useful translations, if understood to have an evaluative meaning distinct from the descriptive word "prostitute." Although "promiscuous" can generally be seen as synonymous with this meaning of "harlot" as unregulated behavior, "harlot" more effectively conveys the designations related to *zenut* and female experience: In a biblical setting both men and women can act promiscuously (*"like* a harlot"), but only women *are* harlots. The English words "harlot" and "harlotry" more clearly convey the female connotation of the Hebrew terms.

The central significance of the concept of harlotry for Hosea and other literary prophets is indicated by the frequency of its use in comparison with other biblical writings. Forms of the verb *zanah* ("to act like a harlot") occur eighty-four times in the whole of the Hebrew Bible. Of those eighty-four references, fifty-one are in the Latter Prophets. Hosea uses a form of *zanah* twenty times.

The importance of harlotry in the first three chapters of Hosea is in connection with the portrayal of Gomer. As Andersen and Freedman have observed, Gomer is characterized as a harlot because of her adulterous and idolatrous behavior, not because she may or may not have been a prostitute.[21] The nature of her harlotry is depicted as involving relationships with human males other than Hosea, as well as participating in Canaanite ritual activity: that is, relationships with male gods other than Yahweh. In these actions, Gomer is used as a representation of the people of Israel in their apostasy and disobedience to God. The interweaving of these themes and the underlying analogy is evident in Hosea 2:15:

> I will punish her for the feast days of the *ba'alim* [Canaanite gods]
>   when she burned incense to them
>   and decked herself with her rings and jewelry,
>   and went after her lovers,
>   and forgot me.

The specific representation of Israel and Yahweh as a woman and a man in a marital relationship has several implications. As discussed earlier, marriage in ancient Israel was in no sense a partnership of equals. The sexes of Gomer and Hosea and their respective behavior are not a random representation but a reflection and reinforcement of cultural perceptions. Hence, Hosea's metaphor has both theological and social meaning. With regard to theological understanding, it indicates that God has the authority of possession and control over Israel that a husband has over a wife. The reverse of the representation is a view of human males as being analogous to Yahweh, while women are comparable to the people, who, by definition, are subservient to Yahweh's will. In a dualistic division between the divine (spiritual) and human (material) spheres of experience, men are categorized as belonging to the former, while women are assigned to the latter.

The positive role of the male (Yahweh/Hosea) in relationship to the female (Israel/Gomer) is evident throughout chapters 1—3. Hosea takes the positive initiative of marrying Gomer, while she behaves negatively in committing adulterous and idolatrous acts. Similarly, Yahweh promises to rectify Israel's disobedience and apostasy by positive action: "I will betroth you to me in faithfulness, and you will know Yahweh" (Hos. 2:21–22).

Another aspect of the perceived female negativity is apparent in the passages describing Gomer/Israel's reliance on her human/divine lovers for sustenance (Hos. 2:7). In condemning this behavior, Hosea asserts that Yahweh is the true provider:

> For she did not know that it was I
> who gave her the grain and the wine and the oil,
> and multiplied unto her silver and gold,
> which they used for Ba'al.
>
> (Hosea 2:10–11)

These passages emphasize female passivity and dependence upon male support. They also ignore, and thus serve to deny, the female role in the provision of food and clothing. The underlying implication is that males nurture females, a reversal of (at least certain aspects of) social reality. A similar reversal seems apparent in Hosea's later depiction of Israel's ingratitude (Hos. 11:1–4; Gen. 2:23) [106].

Gomer's depiction involves her identification with the land, as well as the people, of Israel:

> Let her put away her harlotries from her face,
>   and her adulteries from between her breasts,
> lest I strip her naked
>   and make her as in the day she was born,
> and make her like a wilderness,

> and set her like a parched land,
> and slay her with thirst.
> (Hosea 2:4–5)

On one level this passage describes retribution for harlotrous behavior. As a polemic against Canaanite religion, it deftly sets promiscuity in opposition to fertility and echoes the connection made in Hosea 1:2 between human harlotry and the land. Later in the book, Hosea emphasizes Yahweh's control of fertility in general and female reproductive capability in particular:

> Ephraim's glory will fly away like a bird—
> no birth, no pregnancy, no conception.
> Even if they bring up children,
> I will bereave them until none is left.
> Woe to them
> when I depart from them!
>
> . . . .
>
> Give them, O Yahweh—
> what will you give?
> Give them a miscarrying womb
> and dry breasts.
> (Hosea 9:12, 14)

As in chapter 2, infertility is the result of turning to Canaanite deities for fertility. Reproduction is also clearly the province of Yahweh, divorced from any control of power on the part of women.

In addition to the punishments of deprivation and possible death due to Gomer/Israel for her harlotry, Hosea also describes her public humiliation:

> Now I will uncover her shame
> in the sight of her lovers,
> and no one will rescue her from my hand.
> (Hosea 2:12)

Although the prophet only makes specific use of a female personification of Israel in the first few chapters of Hosea, it is clear throughout the book that his underlying concern is to contrast Yahweh's positive (male) fidelity with Israel's negative (female) harlotry. In so doing, he introduces the themes of the degradation of females and their identification with the land and denies their positive role in human reproduction and nurturance. In his use of the cultural paradigm of marriage as an analogy for the relationship between Yahweh and Israel, Hosea transforms the earlier, material understanding of nonmarital sexuality into an ethical transgression. Or, rather, Hosea witnesses to that historical transition. Whether or not his actual analogy is unique, the efficacy of his prophecy was dependent upon his ability to convey his message to the people of his time. Hence, his using *zenut* (and other related terms) to indicate not only prostitution or apostasy but also adultery and infidelity generally—in other words, harlotry—indicates that this was a perception shared by others around him.

In summarizing Hosea's use of female sexual imagery, we may note indications of an objectified view of female experience as separate from and negative in relationship to male experience. Discussing the political developments of the late eighth century B.C.E. in relation to Hosea's perspective, Andersen and Freedman point out their powerful impact:

> For the first time the threat of national destruction was serious and real, and captivity loomed for the survivors of the impending disaster. Loss of the land and the end of the state were not remote and theoretical possibilities but present and impending realities.[22]

Thus, while the prophecies of Hosea involve a condemnation of the social inequities that developed with the growing prosperity of the monarchical period, they also relate to an experience of disparity between expectation and reality which goes beyond social structure.

The relationship between these historical events and the use of female sexual imagery is illuminated by feminist theoretical considerations. As the development of dualistic perspectives in biblical thought has yet to be adequately explored, it is impossible to determine the extent to which the eighth century represents a point of transition from earlier periods. Nevertheless, there appears to be evidence of an intellectual framework focused on separation between categories previously seen as interrelated. One basis of this perspective may have been a growing material separation between rich and poor, the powerful and the powerless, in Israelite society. Another discrepancy central to prophetic thought is the perceived separation between ritual and ethical action, perhaps related to the centralization and consolidation of religious power on the part of the male Jerusalem priesthood.

To the extent that these separations became generalized into a broader dualistic view of experience, it is possible to understand the development of a perceived dichotomy between female and male human nature. The emergence of objectified female imagery in Hosea and the other literary prophets can be seen as related to the intellectual and psychological disruptions caused by political events. The eventual conquest of Israel involved not only an assertion of the military weakness of the nation but also a significant challenge to previous understanding of the relationship between Yahweh and the people of Israel. The sense of separation from divine protection may have entailed what seemed a basic reversal of right order: The poeple who were supposed to be superior under the aegis of divine power were proven inferior and rendered powerless. Certainly part of the prophets' response to this problem was a reinterpretation of the relationship between Yahweh and Israel. Another aspect of their reaction may have been to assert their personal and collective dignity as men over against a negative characterization and restriction of women.

A central issue for contemporary religious feminists is the extent to which the use of these (and other) biblical writings continues to so define women in our own societies. The use of feminist theory gives us a framework in which to discuss that issue constructively. For some, understanding the historical setting of prophetic texts may provide a perspective of "moral realism" which allows them to be read as sacred writing. For others, the "pornographic" nature of female objectification may demand that such texts not be declared "the word of God" in a public setting. In discussing these issues we will certainly emerge with new questions and challenges as well. As difficult as the process may seem, it is one that may allow us to redefine our relationship not only to the text but also to our own histories and communities in ways which fully acknowledge female experience.

8

Every Two Minutes:
Battered Women
and Feminist Interpretation

Susan Brooks Thistlethwaite

All day long, every day, women are verbally intimidated, battered, injured, and killed by the men they live with. If, as Susan Brownmiller has said, "rapists are the shock troops of patriarchy," then batterers are the army of occupation. This chapter is concerned with the way in which this climate of violence that touches women's lives affects biblical interpretations.

All women live with male violence. A survey conducted by the National Division of the United Methodist Church's Program of Ministries with Women in Crisis in 1980 and 1981 indicates that one in every twenty-seven United Methodist women had been raped, one in every thirteen had been physically abused by her husband, one in every four had been verbally or emotionally abused. Of the respondents, both male and female, one in nine knew of a close friend or relative who had been raped, one in six knew of physical abuse, one in five knew of emotional abuse.[1]

While the authors are aware of the limitations of their survey, as a random sampling of Protestants the survey seems to indicate that even scratching the surface of women's lives reveals the daily presence of violence.

The authors also observed, "Denial runs deep." Their report has met with "disbelief and an amazing capacity to rationalize the findings."[2] Denial is the way to the continuation of the abuse of women. Consciousness of the violence against women with which we all live every day is the beginning of its end.

A feminist biblical interpretation must have this consciousness at its center. The Christian scriptures are inextricably interwoven with this history of the belief systems which support the view of women as scapegoats. In *Violence Against Women,* Emerson and Russell Dobash have a chapter on the relationship of biblical material to the problem of spouse abuse, in which they call women "the appropriate victim." They believe this problem requires intensive examination of history for the structures that support the legitimization of wife as victim.

> The seeds of wife beating lie in the subordination of females and in their subjection to male authority and control. This relationship between women and men has been institutionalized in the structure of the patriarchal family and is supported by the economic and political institutions and by a belief system, *including a religious one,* that makes such relationships seem natural, morally just, sacred.[3]

There is apparent division over the question of whether the location of the authority (warrant, cause, justification) of a feminist interpretation of the Bible is in the text or in women's experience. I believe it is impossible to make this distinction with any clarity because women's experience in Western culture has been shaped by the biblical materials, and the biblical materials were shaped by a patriarchal culture [145–146].

Following a presentation I gave on the Bible and battered women in New York in October 1982, one member of the audience raised the question, "Why deal with the Bible at all?" But as anyone who works with abused women knows, this is not an option. Battered women frequently bring their religious beliefs to the process of working through a battering relationship. Phone calls to shelters often begin with the phrase, "I'm a Bible-believing Christian, but ..." We begin to develop a feminist interpretation because the Bible is a part of the fabric of the oppression of battered women [129].

In the early 1970s I became involved as a pastor counseling abused women. I received calls from some women who were experiencing abuse but were reluctant to try to change their situation because they had been told the teaching of the Bible prohibited their protest. I organized Bible studies with some of these women, and I have continued this work in several locations. Many of the examples that follow are from such groups.

Feminist Method

A feminist method does not always come first chronologically. In Elisabeth Schüssler Fiorenza's landmark work *In Memory of Her: A Feminist Reconstruction of Christian Origins,* method appears first in the volume, but it does not come first in the development of her thought. It was living with the texts themselves in the midst of the contemporary women's movement that shaped her method of investigation. Precisely because it is a method of investigation, it is a process for discovery of what has been hidden.

Moreover, a history of the *use* of biblical materials must become a part of the interpretation. John Cobb has noted that critical study recognizes, and indeed emphasizes, the socio-historical context in which the text functioned in the early church.[4] Feminist biblical interpretation has added a recognition of the patriarchal context in which the text functioned. But the text is still functioning, so to speak, and the patriarchal view that formed part of the formulation of the text is in turn supporting and supported by the text. All that history must become part of a feminist interpretation of the Bible.

Likewise, the origin of women's suspicions of the biblical interpretation of their situation is *both* the text *and* their life experience. Method emerges in this process of interrogation between text and experience. The key is that this process of interrogation proceeds over time.

Work with abused women is a process of support in which women who are physically safe, perhaps for the first time in many years, find self-esteem through affirmations of the gifts of women, through taking control of their lives, and through claiming their anger and finding in that anger a source of strength to act and to change. This process takes time. It cannot happen overnight.

Likewise, the development of a feminist method of biblical interpretation takes time. In Western philosophy, thought has been deemed a timeless, eternal absolute. But if that were the case, nothing new would ever emerge from human consciousness, because it would have to emerge full-blown. Plato wrestled with this problem in the *Meno* and decided that the way we come to know anything new is by remembering it from a formerly perfect state of knowledge before birth. Today we follow an investigative, scientific model of deduction, which holds that thoughts proceed from first principles toward a logical conclusion. This is the grip of positivism, which has held us in obeisance to science for more than two centuries.

In fact, it appears more likely that we think by analogy. When we want to ask about the unknown, we ask, "What is it like?" We learn something new both from the similarity and from the dissimilarity. The tension of the dissimilarity probes us to ask again. Thought moves by analogy and it moves through time. We have to live with something for a while before we can move on.

Over time, women come to varying levels of interpretation of biblical materials. Each of these levels is possible with the whole corpus, and all are necessary in order to deal with the varying attitudes toward women within the Bible.

The Liberation in the Text: Finding Self-esteem

The support given by programs and shelters is essential so that an abused woman can begin to see her life in a new way. Through her research, Lenore Walker has described the battered woman as follows:

1. Has low self-esteem.

2. Believes all the myths about battering relationships.

3. Is a traditionalist about the home, with strong beliefs in family unity and the prescribed feminine sex-role stereotype.

4. Accepts responsibility for the batterer's actions.

5. Suffers from guilt, yet denies the terror and anger she feels.

6. Presents a passive face to the world but has the strength to manipulate her environment enough to prevent further violence.

7. Has severe stress reactions, with psychophysiological complaints.

8. Uses sex as a way to establish intimacy.

9. Believes no one will be able to help her resolve her predicament except herself.[5]

Abused women who receive support begin to learn that they have self-worth and to experience their anger as legitimate. Yet these women believe what they have been taught the Bible says about their situations: that women are inferior in status before husband and God and deserving of a life of pain. One woman said, "God punished women more" (see Gen. 3:16) [114].

Frequently, women with strong religious backgrounds have the most difficulty in accepting that the violence against them is wrong. They believe what they have been taught, that resistance to this injustice is unbiblical and unchristian. Christian women are supposed to be meek, and claiming rights for oneself is committing the sin of pride. But as soon as battered women who hold rigidly traditional religious beliefs begin to develop an ideological suspicion that this violence against them is wrong, they react against it.

In workshops for persons who work with abused women, I have found that most social workers, therapists, and shelter personnel view religious beliefs as uniformly reinforcing passivity and tend to view religion, both traditional Christianity and Judaism, as an obstacle to a woman's successful handling of abuse. Unfortunately, they also say that many strongly religious women cease attending shelters and groups for abused women when these beliefs are attacked.

For women whose religious beliefs include extremely literal interpretations of the Bible as the norm, no authority except that of the Bible itself can challenge the image contained in these texts of woman as silent, subordinate, bearing her children in pain, and subject to the absolute authority of her husband . Yet in Bible study groups, these women can learn that the scriptures are much more on their side than they dared hope. They can become suspicious of a biblical exegesis that is a power play used against them. The process of critical interpretation is often painful and wrenching, because new ways of looking at the Bible have to be learned. But it is also affirming, because one is telling abused women, "You have a right both to your religious beliefs and to your self-esteem."

The core insight with which to begin such a process of interpretive suspicion is that the Bible is written from the perspective of the powerless.[6] The people of Israel, God's chosen, are a ragged band of runaway slaves. God, by identifying *this* people as chosen, is revealed as a God who sides with those who are out of power. It may be that to be out of power is a continuing metaphor in scripture for those who are especially valued by God.

Several types of texts have proved especially helpful to abused women. The theme of God's care for widows and orphans can be helpful in demonstrating that those who are oppressed by societal structures are especially dear to God. A widow in Israel was effectually without economic support and a nonperson in the eyes of that society. The children of a widow, because they lacked this economic support, were considered orphans. God's judgment on those who would afflict any woman or child was especially severe (Ex. 22:2–24).

Yet this does not mean that the impoverished condition of widows and orphans is legitimated because of God's care. God's identification with the oppressed helps them to value themselves as God values them and to recognize that their oppression is unjust. God does not want meek acceptance of oppression.

In *Liberation Preaching,* Justo and Catherine Gonzalez note, "God seems to choose those who have been made to feel like outcasts and then gives them a new sense of self-worth. God vindicates them in the eyes of their former oppressors."[7] This theme of the vindication of the powerless is a constant one in the Hebrew scriptures (see 1 Sam. 2:1–10). It is to be contrasted with the sinful arrogance of the powerful, who believe themselves secure in their own strength (see Psalm 73).

It is essential to see that the ministry of Jesus of Nazareth continued this identification of the chosen of God with the poor. Jesus announced his ministry as one who proclaimed "release to the captives, and recovering of sight to the blind, to set at liberty those who are oppressed, to proclaim the acceptable year of the Lord" (Luke 4:18–20).

Jesus included women in his ministry and ministered to their distress, both spiritual and socioeconomic. The striking amount of biblical material that recounts Jesus' special regard for women, despite androcentric reaction, was the beginning point for the development of a feminist interpretation of the Bible.

Examples of Jesus' care for women are seen in the story of the widow's mite (Luke 21:1–4; 15:8–10), the forgiveness of the prostitute who has faith (Mark 14:3–9), the healing of the woman with the bloody flux (Luke 8:43–48), and the defense of Mary's right to discipleship (John 4:16–30) [57, 58].

Raymond E. Brown has entertained the idea that the crucial role women play in discipleship and apostolic witness is evidence of female leadership in the Johannine community. Jesus' public ministry begins and ends with a story about women: Mary, the mother of Jesus, and Mary Magdalene. Several times, stories of the discipleship of women and that of men are paired: The faithfulness of Nicodemus is paired with the insight of the Samaritan woman; the christological confession of Peter is paralleled by that of Martha. Women's roles in the Fourth Gospel placed them as intimate disciples, those whom Jesus loved (Martha and Mary)

> In researching the evidence of the Fourth Gospel, one is still surprised to see to what extent in the Johannine community women and men were already on an equal level in the Good Shepherd. This seems to have been a community where in the things that really mattered in the following of Christ there was no difference between male and female—a Pauline dream (Gal. 3:28) that was not completely realized in the Pauline communities.[8]

Yet the text with which many abused women find the most identification is John 7:53—8:11. Jesus' defense of the woman who would have been stoned (abused) for adultery, omitted in many manuscripts, including the earliest ones, appears to be an authentic incident in the life of Jesus. Some interpreters have argued that this pericope was not originally part of the Gospel of John. Yet the extraordinary position of women in this Gospel may be a reason for its later inclusion.

Whether or not the woman has already been tried, she is on the verge of execution, having been caught in the act of adultery. Adultery for Jewish women could consist merely in speaking to a male alone. Her crime is not specified beyond that text. But somehow she has transgressed patriarchal grounds.

Textual interpretation usually overlooks the woman's situation and stresses that the scribes and Pharisees wanted to put Jesus to the test and were looking for grounds on which to accuse him.[9] But women who have suffered physical violence hear that whatever human law or custom may legitimate violence against women, it cannot stand face to face with the revelation of God's affirmation of all humanity. Many abused women would echo the joy of the woman who exclaimed, "That's right! He [Jesus] broke the law for her!"

Liberation of the Text: Taking Control

Some biblical material that appears not to address women, or even appears hostile to them, can be reworked to bring out liberating themes for abused women. The opinion of women that prevailing androcentric interpretation of the Bible is wrong, coupled with the emphasis in a major portion of the biblical materials themselves on God's identification with the oppressed, creates critical interpretation. Consciousness-raising for these women has provided the essential catalyst: the insight that women are included in the category of the poor, the oppressed, and the outcast. Moving from that critical standpoint, women can begin to examine and reinterpret these texts, imagining new relationships between the texts and their experience.

An especially useful text is Luke 9:1–5, which ends, "And wherever they do not receive you, when you leave [there] shake off the dust from your feet as a testimony against them." One of the crucial issues for abused women is the psychological and physical intimidation they experience, which prevents them from leaving. Shelters and safe houses can begin to help with the fear of destitution and further violence faced by a woman who contemplates leaving. But there are psychological factors as well, which include religious sanctions against a woman's "breaking up the home."

> What kind of people are my children going to become, seeing us or hearing us live this way? Will my son abuse his wife or girlfriend as he's seen his father do? Will my daughter live in fear and dread of every man she meets? For *them,* if not for me, I've got to do something. But instead, I stay, and stay, and stay for what seems like an eternal hell. I can't see my way out. I'm fearful of losing family respect for my failed marriage, *afraid of censure about my religious convictions,* fearful of a terrible reputation with my own friends (the few who are left). Finally I become obsessed

with a fear of losing my respect for myself, and for my sanity—what's left of it.[10]

Because abused women experience themselves as out of control of their lives, part of working with them involves attempts to take control. One of the major obstacles to women's hearing the permission to leave where they are not valued is that they do not identify themselves with the disciples.

Disciples are followers of Jesus who hear the Word and do it (Mark 8:34–35). By this definition, the Synoptic Gospels agree that women were among the most faithful of Jesus' disciples, remaining at the foot of the cross even when others had fled. Jesus appeared first to women and commissioned them to tell of his resurrection, the central fact of the "good news," to the other disciples (Matt. 28:10; Mark 16:7; Luke 24:8–9).

The Roman Catholic Church has emphasized the absence of women among the twelve as indicative of Jesus' preference for male leadership.[11] While the New Testament authors are not uniformly in agreement on the role of the twelve, the theological function of the twelve is to represent the twelve tribes of Israel. In this way they provide a bridge between the Israelite past and the hoped-for future in which all Jews and Gentiles would be united as the People of God. The twelve thus have a largely symbolic role, not an administrative one, as evidenced by the fact that they were not replaced by the church after their deaths.[12]

Much of the New Testament material leads one to believe that the circle around Jesus was in fact quite fluid and did include women. Another title for Jesus' followers throughout his ministry is apostles. Generally, the term "apostle" is thought to refer to the twelve, a point of view held by the framers of the Vatican Declaration. On the contrary: It is a much wider circle, according to some New Testament writers. Junia, considered a woman by John Chrysostom, is named by Paul as "outstanding among the apostles" (Rom. 16:7, NIV). The "apostle" Paul, of course, was not a member of the twelve at all (see Gal. 1:11ff.).

It is therefore quite reasonable to decide that women were included in the most intimate circle around Jesus and that their inclusion was deliberate on his part. We begin to see how this text can be heard as addressing women. Power and authority are given to those who hear the Word of God and do it, the disciples. Women can claim this power and authority to heal their situation. One woman, reading the text in this way, remarked, "I thought that you always had to turn the other cheek."

For too long we have neglected the healing and casting out of demons that occurs so frequently in biblical materials in favor of discussions focused solely around the miraculous. But for abused women, women who study the Bible with bloodied noses, bruised ribs, and broken limbs, healing has a concrete and immediate reference. Likewise, the demonic has a concrete reference for those who have experienced the cycle of violence that builds in the home of an abuser.[13]

Women are not named in scripture as among the twelve. But women can learn to imagine themselves in the text on the basis of other textual material that does affirm women (such as women's discipleship) and on the basis of their own experience, which shows that they have been the ones to hear the Word of God and do it. This type of imagining challenges traditional interpretation, which has ignored women who are actually in the text or whose presence is implied by the text, and moves interpretation to a new level of engagement with the contemporary life of the church.

The Liberation from the Text: Claiming Anger

Recently I have been conducting Bible study groups composed primarily of Catholic women over forty. Biblical material has not formed the religious framework for their acceptance of battering. Rather, it has been the church and its teaching about the role of women, divorce, and contraception that has provided religious legitimation for battering. Biblical study with these women has proceeded in a different manner because they did not regard the text as the primary religious authority in their lives. Rather, they were willing to enter into a suspicion of the many texts we examined that seemed to legitimize violence against women. These women found that they could not always trust the text or its traditional interpretations and that some of the texts are "harmful to their health" [55, 130].

Ephesians 5:21–23 is a very difficult passage for abused women struggling to find self-respect and some control over their lives. A preliminary study of this passage modifies extreme misinterpretation by demonstrating that to be "subject" (v. 21) does not mean specifically subject to physical violence: "For no man ever hates his own flesh, but nourishes and cherishes it, as Christ does the church" (v. 29). Husbands are admonished to love their wives "as their own bodies" (v. 28).

But physical violence is not the only form of abuse. Verbal intimidation, economic deprivation, and deliberate humiliation also characterize the violent relationship. One woman reported that her husband would deliberately keep her from arriving at family parties on time and then make her apologize to her relatives for being so late. This type of subjection appears compatible with the Ephesians passage, since only wives are admonished to "respect" their spouses.

Liberation from this text requires a recognition of its location within the biblical materials and of the function this particular emphasis in Ephesians played in the history of the church. In the pseudo-Pauline epistles, a shift away from the egalitarian ethos of the Jesus movement can be observed. Ephesians was written about the same time as Colossians, another epistle where the subjection of wives to husbands is emphasized. This is the first of the household duty codes, a series of exhortations to obedience in the households of the early Christian communities.

In Colossians 3:11, women are left out of the otherwise complete repetition of the baptismal formula of Galatians 3:28: "Here there cannot be Greek and Jew, circumcised and uncircumcised, barbarian, Scythian, slave, free man, but Christ is all, and all in all." "Neither male nor female" seems to belong to an earlier vision of human equality in Christ.

In Ephesians the household duty codes are limited to the relation of husbands and wives, combined with a theology of Christ and the church. This tends to reinforce the cultural notion of submission contained in the household duty codes with a theological legitimation of dominance and submission in the household of God. While the negative exhortation of Colossians ("Do not be harsh" to your wives) is softened ("Love" your wives), the inferior position of both wives and the church is cemented.

This is not the only pattern for divine–human relationships in the scripture. It is a pattern developed in response to social criticism of the newfound freedom of Christians, especially as this was reflected in the behavior of Christian wives and slaves. Other patterns exist, such as Galatians 3:28, and these can be drawn upon to critique patriarchal patterns such as Ephesians 5:21–23. The religious sanction in the household codes for the submission of women is a primary legitimation of wife abuse and must be challenged by women in order for them to gain some control over their own lives. A woman relates the traditional response of clergy:

> Well, he spoke to both of us and he sat down for about an hour and he spoke about our financial situation and how having a child affected a marriage and things like that. Then he would bring in the vows of marriage—"to love, honor, and obey until death do us part." And I argued on the point of obeying because I feel, I felt at that time, to obey, it's all

right in certain principles but you cannot obey all your life. I mean, if I asked him to stop gambling he would not obey me, but I have to obey all his rules. The minister would not talk about that fact.[14]

On the contrary, we must begin to talk about obedience and the role it has played in the cultural accommodation of religion to social mores, particularly to patriarchy. We must find strength to reject this notion of obedience to male authority in claiming our anger at the suffering that women have experienced in obedience.

A final text to consider within this rubric of liberation from the text involves a more subtle perception of the patriarchal violence against women that is in the biblical material. Genesis 2:21–24 is such a text.

Although Phyllis Trible has dealt with this text creatively in suggesting ways it can be understood as a basis of equality between woman and man, feminist interpretation must also recognize that the history of control of women's bodies is at stake in this text and must become part of its interpretation.[15] In the development of patriarchy, a very important issue has been control of women's abilities to procreate. The ability of women's bodies to create life has resulted in awe, fear, and the desire to control this power. While Freud may have discovered penis envy, womb envy has also played a role in human history.

This story is apparent in Genesis 2. A woman is born from a man in contrast to every other human birth. Perhaps, too, this interpretation of the first birth is also meant to symbolize control over woman's abilities to make decisions about whether to bear a child. From an early period the church has attempted to curtail knowledge of contraception and abortion. Puritanical Protestants led a late-nineteenth-century campaign to pass laws making contraceptive knowledge a crime. The current "Right to Life" movement is ecumenical in that its adherents are both Catholics and Evangelical/Fundamentalist Protestants. These movements are attacks on female autonomy, which threatens patriarchal power at its core.

A Maryland woman who was severely abused over many years told me that when she complained after some attacks that she had sustained injuries, her husband would retort that "your bones are my bones—just like it says in the Bible." Less explicit reinforcement of patterns of domination and submission that legitimate violence against women can be found in interpretations of this text. Walter Brueggemann argues in the *Catholic Biblical Quarterly* that this text "suggests nothing of the superiority of the male as is often suggested." But Brueggemann correctly connects this text to marriage metaphors for divine–human relationship, such as "the Image of

God and his [sic] bride Israel."[16] He then rightly draws the important analogy between Genesis 2:18–23 and Ephesians 5:21–33:

> The same imagery in Paul [Ephesians 5:21–23] is illuminated. The relation of Christ and his bride-church is grounded in a commonality of concern, loyalty, and responsibility which is pledged to endure through weakness and strength.[17]

But the metaphor of patriarchal marriage for divine–human relationship is not one of mutuality; it is an image of dominance and subordination in that cultural context. Likewise, tying marriage to the divine–human relationship clearly divinizes male superiority in that relationship.

Brueggemann's interpretation of Genesis 2:18–23 illustrates the limits of a biblical interpretation that does not take a nuanced approach to the materials. There is much affirmation of women within the biblical materials, but grounds for violence against women exist as well, along with much material in between. This material has shaped cultural attitudes toward women. But contemporary experience also shapes our interpretation of the text [91, 92].

Feminist biblical interpretation for women who live with male violence is a healing process that develops over time. It involves claiming self-esteem, taking control, and owning one's anger. Women's relationships to biblical materials need to undergo the same type of healing process. As Adrienne Rich has observed, "We have lived with violence far too long."[18]

Part III

Feminist Critical Principles

9

Feminist Interpretation:
A Method of Correlation

Rosemary Radford Ruether

It has been frequently said that feminist theology and theory of interpretation draw upon women's experience as a source of knowledge. It has not been entirely clear what this means. It is generally assumed by traditional theology that any experience, let alone "women's experience," is merely a subjective and culture-bound source of ideas and cannot be compared with the objectivity of scripture, which discloses the "Word of God" outside of, over, and against the subjectivity and sinful impulses of human experience. As a narrow and contemporary source, experience cannot compare with the accumulated weight of theological tradition. It is sheer impertinence to suggest that "women's experience" can be used to judge scripture and theological tradition.

Such a response, aside from its trivializing of women's persons, misunderstands the role of human experience in the formation of scripture and theological tradition. Human experience is both the starting point and the ending point of the circle of interpretation. Codified tradition both reaches back to its roots in experience and is constantly renewed through the test of experience. Experience includes experience of the divine and experience of oneself, in relationship to society and the world, in an interacting dialectic. Received symbols, formulas, and laws are either authenticated or not through their ability to illuminate and interpret existence in a way that is experienced as meaningful. Systems of authority try to reverse this relationship and make received tradition dictate both what may be experienced and how it may be interpreted. But the relationship is the opposite. If the symbol does not speak authentically to experience, it becomes dead and is discarded or altered to provide new meaning [44].

Religious traditions begin with breakthrough experiences that shed revelatory light on contemporary events so as to transform them into paradigms of ultimate meaning. These experiences, such as the exodus experience or the resurrection experience, are the primary data of the religious tradition. But such experiences, however new and transformative, do not interpret themselves. They are always interpreted in the context of an accumulated heritage of symbols and codes, which are already available to provide touchstones of meaning. The new revelatory experience becomes meaningful by being related to this heritage, and also it allows the contemporary community to transform, revise, and recombine the traditional touchstones of meaning in new ways, which allows the new experience to become a new insight into the ultimate nature of things.

Just as the foundational revelatory experience is available only in a transformative dialectic between experience and accumulated interpretive keys, so it, in turn, becomes an interpretive key which interacts with and continues to be meaningful through its ability to make ongoing experience of the individual in the community meaningful. This key then continues to live because it is able to continue to make contemporary experience meaningful, and it itself is constantly revised or reinterpreted through this same process. Traditions die when a new generation is no longer able to reappropriate the foundational paradigm in a meaningful way; when it is experienced as meaningless or even as demonic: that is, disclosing a meaning that points to false or inauthentic life. Thus if the cross of Jesus would be experienced by women as pointing them only toward continued victimization and not redemption, it would be perceived as false and demonic in this way, and women could no longer identify themselves as Christians.

Women's Experience and Feminist Hermeneutics

What is new about feminist hermeneutics, then, is not the category of experience as a context of interpretation but rather the appeal to *women's experience.* It is precisely women's experience that has been shut out of hermeneutics and theological reflection in the past. This has been done by forbidding women to study and then to teach and preach the theological tradition. Women have not been able to bring their own experience into the public formulation of the tradition. Not only have women been excluded from shaping and interpreting the tradition from their own experience, but the tradition has been shaped and interpreted against them. The tradition has been shaped to justify their exclusion. The traces of their presence have been suppressed and lost from the public memory of the community. The androcentric bias of the male interpreters of the tradition, who regard maleness as normative humanity, not only erase women's presence in the past history of the community but silence even the questions about their absence. One is not even able to remark upon or notice women's absence, since women's silence and absence is the norm.

Thus the criticism of the tradition in the context of women's experience does not merely add another point of view to the prevailing one. Women's experience explodes as a critical force, exposing classical theology, including its foundational tradition in scripture, as shaped by male experience rather than human experience. Women's experience makes the androcentric bias of the original formulations and ongoing interpretations of the tradition visible, rather than hidden behind the mystifications of divine authority. It throws the universality of the claims of the tradition into question.

What is meant by women's experience? Surely all women do not have the same experiences. There are many variations in the consciousness of women, shaped by different cultural contexts and life experiences. How then can one generalize about women's experience? Is one suggesting that women, because of biological differences from men, possess a distinctively "feminine" psychology, and that it is this distinctive psychology they bring to biblical hermeneutics?

Biological differences are not completely irrelevant. Women, as persons who live in and through a female body, have some distinctive experiences of the world that men do not have. A woman who has experienced her bodily rhythms in menstruation, or who has borne and suckled a child, feels some things which males have never experienced. One need not reject out of hand that women may bring such experiences to the interpretive task. One finds, for example, in the writings of women mystics, the use of experiences of birthing and suckling that draw on such women's experiences as paradigms of divine–human relationships.

However, in this context we are not talking about women's experience primarily in terms of experiences created by biological differences in themselves but, rather, women's experiences created by the social and cultural appropriation of biological differences in a male-dominated society. In such a society, women experience even their biological differences in ways filtered and biased by male dominance and by their own marginalization and inferiorization. Menstruation and childbirth are interpreted to them as pollution, over against a male-controlled sacred sphere, for example, which alienates them from a positive understanding of their own bodily experiences [88,

89]. Insofar as they appropriate their own experiences, such as the experience of menstruation, as a positive and creative rhythm of ebb and flow, they must do so in contradiction to the male hermeneutic of their own experience imposed upon them by the dominant culture. Their positive appropriation of their experience from their own vantage point becomes a covert critical counterculture over against the official culture.

Women in patriarchal culture are surrounded by messages that negate or trivialize their existence. Their bodily sexual presence is regarded as a dangerous threat to male purity and, at the same time, as a justification for constant verbal and physical abuse. They experience their bodies as constantly vulnerable to assault and are told, at the same time, that they deserve such assault because they "cause" it by their sexual presence. Similarly, women find their own viewpoints and judgments of events trivialized, and this trivialization is justified on the grounds that women are inherently stupid, uninformed, lacking in authority, and incapable of forming significant understandings. Thus they are alienated from their own minds, from being able to trust their own perceptions. These judgments upon the woman's body and mind are, in turn, used to justify women's exclusion from cultural opportunities and leadership. Women are asked to accept this, too, as normal, natural, divinely sanctioned [99].

By women's experience as a key to hermeneutics or theory of interpretation, we mean precisely that experience which arises when women become critically aware of these falsifying and alienating experiences imposed upon them as women by a male-dominated culture. Women's experience, in this sense, is itself a grace event, an infusion of liberating empowerment from beyond the patriarchal cultural context, which allows them to critique and stand out against these androcentric interpretations of who and what they are. Women begin to name these experiences of negation and trivialization as wrong and contrary to their authentic humanity. They begin to find an alternative stand in their own shared reflection on this experience from which to judge it. They affirm their own bodies and bodily experiences as good and normative for them, rather than deviant; their own feelings and thoughts as intelligent and healthy, rather than stupid. From this empowerment to self-affirmation, they are able to place under judgment—and also progressively to free themselves from—that culture which negates them.

It is this process of the critical naming of women's experience of androcentric culture that we refer to when we say that women's experience is an interpretive key for feminist theology. Women's experience, then, implies a conversion experience through which women get in touch with, name, and judge their experiences of sexism in patriarchal society. Not all cultures create exactly the same experiences of sexism, and individual women may have experienced this differently as well. So women do not come to exactly the same criticisms of these experiences or the same conclusions about them. Feminism must leave room for such individual and cross-cultural differences. Nevertheless, patriarchy by its very nature provides enough of a common body of experiences that women, even from different cultures and religions, find commonalities. But this conversation can happen only when women become freed and empowered to criticize the experience of sexism as an unjustified assault upon their beings, rather than accepting it as the norm.

The critique of sexism implies a fundamental principle of judgment. This critical principle of feminist theology is the affirmation of and promotion of the full humanity of women. Whatever denies, diminishes, or distorts the full humanity of women is, therefore, to be appraised as not redemptive. Theologically speaking, this means that whatever diminishes or denies the full humanity of women must be presumed not to reflect the divine or authentic relation to the divine, or to reflect the authentic nature of things, or to be the message or work of an authentic redeemer or a community of redemption [44, 45].

This negative principle also implies the positive principle: What does promote the full humanity of women is of the Holy, does reflect true relation to the divine, is the true nature of things, is the authentic message of redemption and the mission of redemptive community. But the meaning of this positive principle—namely, the full humanity of women—is not fully known. It has not existed in history as we have known it. What we have known is only the negative principle of the denigration and marginalization of women's humanity. But the humanity of women, although diminished, has not been destroyed. It has constantly affirmed itself, albeit at times only in limited and subversive ways. It is the touchstone by which we test and criticize all that diminishes us. In the process we experience our larger potential, which allows us to begin to imagine a world without sexism.

This principle is hardly new. In fact, the correlation of original and authentic human nature (*imago dei*/Christ) over against diminished, fallen humanity has traditionally provided the basic structure of classical Christian theology. The uniqueness of feminist theology is not the critical principle of "full humanity" but that women claim this principle for themselves. Women name themselves as subjects of authentic and full humanity.

In this light, the use of this principle in male theology is perceived to have been corrupted by sexism. By naming males as norms of authentic humanity, women have been scapegoated for sin and marginalized in both original and redeemed humanity. This distorts and turns to the opposite the theological understanding of the created and redeemed image of God. Defined as male humanity against or above women, as ruling-class humanity above servant classes, the *imago dei*/Christ paradigm becomes an instrument of sin rather than a disclosure of the divine and an instrument of grace.

But this also implies that women cannot just reverse the sin of sexism. Women cannot just blame males for historical evil in a way that makes themselves only innocent victims. Women cannot affirm themselves as created in the image of God and as subjects of full human potential in a way that diminishes male humanity. Women, as the denigrated half of the human species, must reach for a continually expanding definition of the inclusive humanity: inclusive of both genders, inclusive of all social groups and races. Any principle of religion or society that marginalizes one group of persons as less than fully human diminishes us all. In rejecting androcentrism (males as norms of humanity), women must also criticize all other forms of chauvinism: making white Westerners the norm of humanity, making Christians the norm of humanity, making privileged classes the norm of humanity. They must also criticize humanocentrism: making humans the norm and "crown" of creation in a way that diminishes other beings in the community of creation. This is not a question of "sameness" but of recognition of value which, at the same time, affirms genuine variety and particularity. It reaches for a new mode of relationship: neither a hierarchical model that diminishes the potential of the "other" nor an "equality" defined by a ruling norm drawn from the dominant group, but rather a mutuality that allows us to affirm different ways of being [144].

The Correlation of Feminist and Biblical Critical Principles

The feminist critique of sexism finds patriarchy not only in contemporary and historical Christian culture but in the Bible. The Bible was shaped by males in a patriarchal culture, so much of its revelatory experiences were interpreted by men from a patriarchal perspective. The ongoing interpretation of these revelatory experiences and their canonization further this patriarchal bias by eliminating traces of female experience or interpreting them in an androcentric way. The Bible, in turn, becomes the authoritative source for the justification of patriarchy in Jewish and Christian society. The feminist critical principle thus demands that women stand outside of and in judgment upon this patriarchal bias of the scriptures. If this were all the Bible is, the principle would also demand that feminism reject the scriptures altogether as normative for its own liberation. The Bible would reveal only a demonic falsification of woman's being; it would not provide touchstones for a liberating alternative.

The Bible can be appropriated as a source of liberating paradigms only if it can be seen that there is a correlation between the feminist critical principle and that critical principle by which biblical thought critiques itself and renews its vision as the authentic Word of God over against corrupting and sinful deformations. It is my contention here that there is such a correlation between biblical and feminist critical principles. This biblical critical principle is that of the prophetic-messianic tradition. By the prophetic-messianic tradition I mean to name not simply a particular body of texts, which then would be understood as standing as a canon within the canon. Rather, what I mean by the prophetic-messianic tradition is a critical perspective and process through which the biblical tradition constantly reevaluates, in new contexts, what is truly the liberating Word of God, over against both the sinful deformations of contemporary society and also the limitations of past biblical traditions, which saw in part and understood in part, and whose partiality may have even become a source of sinful injustice and idolatry [131].

In much of human history, the divine world has been used to sacralize the existing social order. This is done by implying that the gods created the social order as it is, intending some to rule and some to serve. The gods promulgated the laws that codify this social order, and so it reflects their decree. To rebel against it is to rebel against the gods. The patriarchal social order of men over women, masters over slaves, king (or queen) over subjects, nobility over peasants itself is seen as reflecting the cosmic and heavenly order. Hence the divine world is pictured as an immortal imitation of the ruling classes.

This function of religion as sanctification of the existing social order is also found in the Bible. It is reflected particularly in the Levitical codes of the Hebrew scripture and the household codes of the New Testament. But this function of religion as sacred canopy is in contradiction to an alternative perspective, which seems to this author to constitute the distinctive expression of biblical faith. In the prophetic perspective, God speaks through the prophet or prophetess as critic, rather than sanctifier, of the status quo. God's will is revealed as standing in judgment upon the injustices of the way society is being conducted, especially by the wealthy and powerful. This critique of society includes a critique of religion. The spokesperson of God denounces the way in which religion is misused to countenance injustice and to turn away the eyes of the pious from the poor. In the words of Amos 5:21, 24, "I hate, I despise your feasts, and I take no delight in your solemn assemblies. . . . But let justice roll down like waters, and righteousness like an everflowing stream."

This prophetic critique of established structures of injustice, and their religious justifications, creates a reevaluation of the relationship of God—God's power and will in history—toward society. Divine revelation does not buttress, but destabilizes, the ideologies that support the social order. God's prophet points toward an alternative social order, an alternative era of human history, when these wrongs will be righted and a new time of God's peace and justice will reign. This biblical principle of prophetic faith parallels the critical dynamic of feminism, which likewise examines structures of injustice toward women, unmasks and denounces their cultural and religious sanctifications, and points toward an alternative humanity, an alternative society, capable of affirming the personhood of women.

It may be said that this correlation between the biblical critical principle and the feminist critical principle is insufficient, because biblical prophecy does not clearly include sexism and patriarchy in its critique of social injustice. Women, in expanding the prophetic process of denunciation and annunciation to include sexism, do so without biblical authority. In responding to such a justified objection, one must be clear about the sociology of consciousness of all critical prophetic culture. One cannot reify any critical prophetic movement, either in scripture or in modern liberation movements, simply as definitive texts, once and for all established in the past, which then set the limits of consciousness of the meaning of liberation. Rather, the prophetic tradition remains true to itself, to its own impulse and spirit, only by engagement in constant restatement in the context of the issues of justice and injustice in its times [55].

Continuity with the prophetic tradition, then, is not simply restatement of past texts but the constant renewal of the meaning of the prophetic critique itself. This means that prophetic critique is in a constant state of revision by situating itself in contemporary issues and contemporary consciousness of good and evil and by becoming a vehicle for the critical consciousness of groups who have been shut out of the social dialogue in the past. In this process of renewal, one must also examine the limitations of past statements of prophetic consciousness, which have been limited by the social consciousness of their spokespersons. Prophetic critique is renewed both by new critical consciousness of the issues of today and by new perceptions of the limits and deformations of its own past traditions.

Prophetic traditions are limited and become deformed in two ways. First of all, there is always a sociology of consciousness of critical movements. However much the spokespersons of a critical movement intend to speak inclusively of those who are poor and oppressed in the society, their perception of who these people are and what the issues are is limited by their own social context. Prophets are aware of who is hurting them and the groups of people with whom they feel primary bonds. They may be insensitive or oblivious to other oppressed people who are the underside of social systems from which they themselves benefit. Thus the Hebrew scriptures present us with a dynamic and moving language that criticizes the social injustice heaped upon those groups with whom the prophet identifies: the poor rural Israelite farmer over against the rich urbanite, and the enslaved Jewish people over against the great empires of antiquity. But the prophets are oblivious to or justify that enslavement of persons within the Hebrew family itself: namely, women and slaves. At most, their vision of justice for these people extends to an amelioration of the harshness of the system under which they suffer, rather than a real critique of that system itself or an ability to imagine that God is calling for an alternative to it.

One can recognize the same limitations of critical social consciousness in modern liberation movements. Feminism in the West has called for justice for women, but the white middle-class context of feminists has often made them oblivious to the class and race bias of their discernment of injustices and their vision of alternatives. They have often not recognized the way in which the burning issues of social injustice for them touched very little upon the interests and needs of Black or poor women. Or a Christian-based feminism has sometimes sought an affirmation of Christian feminism in a way that made Judaism the scapegoat for patriarchy. And so what appeared to be good news for Christian feminists about "Jesus as a feminist" was experienced as bad news by Jewish feminists [157, Note 1].

One can chart a similar insensitivity to women and to racial minorities in the Marxist left and in Third World liberation theologies. Today, feminists and other liberation movements become more aware of the need for dialogue between movements for emancipation in different social and cultural contexts in order to expand their sensitivities. But no liberation movement can speak the universal critical word about injustice and hope for all time; it always does so within the limitations of its social location. This means not only that an emancipatory movement may notice some oppressed

groups, but not others in its midst, but also that its particular perception of the good news for its suffering poor may justify injustice
against others. The announcement of good news for us is always,
in some sense, bad news for our enemies. But this may be understood either in a more self-critical and open way or in a more
parochial and triumphalistic way, which merely wishes to turn the
tables on one's enemies and reduce them to the same oppression
that one's own people is presently suffering, rather than to construct
a new humanity and society where there are no longer victor and
vanquished.

Not only may the prophetic consciousness be limited and deformed in these ways in its own time and context, but, in the process
of formulating and transmitting prophetic consciousness as tradition, the meaning of early critical consciousness may become deformed by being interpreted in a different social context. Thus what
was once critical consciousness over against established traditions
in one context becomes new self-justification of established hierarchies in another context, which has absorbed a prophetic tradition
as authoritative text for its own religious establishment.

There are many examples of the process of deformation and
renewal of prophetic language within the scriptures, as well as in the
subsequent ecclesiastical appropriation of these texts. For example,
the New Testament conflict with dominant religious authorities of
Judaism operated in the mission of Jesus and the earliest church as
a criticism of fossilized religion and clericalism in order to call
Judaism itself back to its prophetic mission. But when Christianity
became a separate Gentile religion and then the dominant religion
of the Roman Empire, this language of self-criticism was used to
reject Judaism as an inferior religion and to ratify a chauvinistic
triumphalism of church over synagogue.

The language of messianism also can change its meaning in different contexts. Much messianic imagery was drawn originally from
ancient Near Eastern kingship language. This was critically reeval-
uated by the prophets, detached from its ideological justification of
existing kings, and projected on an idealized future hope. This
made messianic language a judgment upon existing kings and a
hope for an alternative social order. But when Christianity became
an imperial religion, this kingship language could be used to sacralize existing Christian monarchs as expressions of divine kingship
and representatives of Christ on earth.

Servanthood language likewise changes its meaning radically in
different contexts. In its use by Jesus, appropriated from the prophetic tradition, it means that God alone is father and king. We,
therefore, are freed from allegiance to human fathers and kings. As

servants of God alone, we are freed from servitude to human hierarchies of power. But when imperial Christianity again lines up these human hierarchies of power as expressions of Christ's reign, then this servanthood language is used to reinforce, in Christ's name, the servitude of subjugated people.

Key to this ideological deformation is the movement of the socioreligious group addressed from powerlessness to power. When religious spokespersons identify themselves as members and advocates of the poor, then the critical-prophetic language rediscovers its cutting edge. When religious spokespersons see themselves primarily as stabilizing the existing social order and justifying its power structure, then prophetic language becomes deformed in the interests of the status quo, becoming a language to sacralize dominant authorities and to preach revenge against former enemies.

One example of reinterpretation of prophetic criticism and hope occurs in Jesus' interpretation of the text of Isaiah 61. This chapter of Isaiah opens with the dramatic announcement of good news to the poor.

> [The LORD] has sent me to bind up the brokenhearted,
> to proclaim liberty to the captives,
>   and the opening of the prison to those who are bound;
> to proclaim the year of the LORD's favor,
>   and the day of [recompense] of our God.
> (Isaiah 61:1–2)

In Isaiah 61 this renewal of the ancient promises of messianic hope is put together with texts that interpret this hope in terms of a nationalistic triumph of Israel over the Gentile nations:

> Aliens shall stand and feed your flocks,
>   foreigners shall be your plowmen and vinedressers;
>
> . . . .
>
> you shall eat the wealth of the nations,
>   and in their riches you shall glory.
> Instead of your shame you shall have a double portion.
> (Isaiah 61:5–7)

In the Lukan version of Jesus' use of this text in the synagogue in Nazareth, we find a dramatic reinterpretation of this message of national triumph. Jesus is portrayed as reading the opening verses of Isaiah and declaring, "Today this scripture has been fulfilled in your hearing" (Luke 4:21). This evokes admiration and praise from the hometown folks. "All spoke well of him, and wondered at the gracious words" (Luke 4:22). But then Jesus launches into an inter-

pretation of the text, and the mood shifts dramatically. He interprets it as good news and healing that will come not to Israel but
to the Gentiles and, indeed, to women and lepers among the Gentiles (Luke 4:25–27). This prophetic reversal of the interpretation
of the text is intended to call the synagogue community to a criticism of their ethnocentric chauvinism and to an opening of their
minds to peoples around them whom they despise. Jesus does not
feel bound to repeat the interpretation of the text found in Isaiah,
but even to reverse it in order to make new critical points that God
is calling people to hear.

However, for Christians today simply to repeat this prophetic
reversal of the Isaiah text would not mean the same thing as it meant
in a Jewish context. Today Christians would easily read Jesus' reinterpretation of Isaiah as a triumphalistic justification of Gentile
Christianity over against an inferior particularism of Judaism. It
would be heard as a word against the Jewish community rather than
a word within and for Israel, calling them to a widening of their
vision. Therefore, if we today were to declare this same text, we too
would have to reinterpret it in order to apply it to the outsiders and
the despised of our time.

We might imagine a preacher in the contemporary church reading the Isaiah text and then doing the following commentary upon
it: "There are many church people all over America who speak
constantly of salvation, but true salvation is only really announced
in those gatherings where women preach hope to women and poor
people against patriarchy; and there are many therapists and healers
in the land, but true healing comes only to those shelters which
women have set up to house battered wives and homeless women
who walk the streets carrying their few possessions in shopping
bags." Such a commentary on the prophetic text in our time, as in
Jesus' time, might well cause the good church folks to rise up in fury
and try to kill us. The feminist interpretation of prophetic critique
as feminist critique thus continues the process of scriptural hermeneutic itself, whereby the text is reinterpreted in the context of
new communities of critical consciousness.

Is this the first time that prophetic critique has been appropriated
by women? Is this the first time that women have claimed the authority to proclaim the good news as the good news of liberation
from patriarchy? We would postulate that wherever women have
heard the good news as the setting at liberty of those who are
oppressed, they have applied it to themselves as women as well. We
postulate this because our affirmation of the full humanity of women
includes the assumption that women themselves have not just
begun to affirm their humanity in modern times but have always

affirmed their humanity. Patriarchal indoctrination of women to accept their own inferiority and triviality has never been complete. Indeed, the constant need of patriarchal culture to reiterate the demand for women's subordination and silence indicates that women have never lost the sense of their own self-worth but have constantly asserted it over against patriarchal commands. Thus the question is not whether women have ever applied the good news to themselves as women, but how and to what extent the records of this feminist hermeneutic have survived the effects of patriarchal erasure of women's self-affirmation from the collective cultural memory.

We can see evidence of such appropriation of the good news to women in the New Testament: for example, in the stories where women among the poor and marginalized hear the good news when the clerical authorities do not; in the records of women's participation in early Christian ministry; and in the vision of a new humanity where "there is neither male nor female" (Gal. 3:28). But we also trace in the New Testament the record of patriarchal erasure of this memory. We need to put the New Testament itself in the context of other early Christian texts, such as the Acts of Paul and Thecla, where Paul is understood by early Christian communities not as telling women to keep silence but as commissioning a woman to preach.

We can trace the ongoing record of women's appropriation of the good news as good news for women in historical records in every generation, such as in the androgynous vision of God of Julian of Norwich and in the scriptural exegesis of Margaret Fell in the seventeenth century, in which "women's preaching" was justified according to the scriptures. We see this record of feminist consciousness in the admonition of Abigail Adams to her husband at the Continental Congress to "remember the Ladies." We see the bold reworking of the Declaration of Independence in the Seneca Falls Women's Rights Convention of 1848, where this foundational text of American emancipation was rewritten as the charter for women's emancipation from patriarchy in church and society.

Thus the question is not whether women have affirmed themselves before or whether they have been able to grasp the good news of male-led prophetic movements as good news for themselves as well. Rather, the question is how did the beginnings of such feminist reinterpretation become stillborn in women's minds? Or, if not stillborn, but brought forth in word, how was this word prevented from being committed to praxis? Or, if committed to praxis, how was it prevented from being written down? Or, if written down, how was the textual record of it lost, or reinterpreted, so that it has been erased from memory? The recovery of our history is the recovery of evidence of all the stages of this repression. It is also the history of the breakthroughs to feminist consciousness that have not been completely erased. Here and there, fragments remain, allowing us to make contact with our sisters of past ages who also heard the good news and claimed it as their own.

The task of feminist hermeneutics today is not only to develop and solidify the principles by which women appropriate the good news as good news of liberation from patriarchy and develop the stories and texts to proclaim this good news. The task of feminist hermeneutics is also to establish this theory of interpretation as normative and indispensable to the understanding of the faith, in seminaries where interpretation is taught and in churches and synagogues where the good news is preached. In short, the task of feminist hermeneutics is not only to do the interpretation of the good news as good news for women but to see to it that the memory of this interpretation will not again be erased from the collective memory of the communities of biblical faith.

IO

The Will to Choose or to Reject: Continuing Our Critical Work

Elisabeth Schüssler Fiorenza

I'm ceded—I've stopped being Theirs—
The name They dropped upon my face
With water, in the country church
Is finished using, now,
And They can put it with my Dolls,
My childhood, and the string of spools,
I've finished threading—too—

Baptized before, without the choice,
But this time, consciously, of Grace—
Unto supremest name—
Called to my Full—The Crescent dropped—
Existence's whole Arc, filled up,
With one small Diadem.

My second Rank—too small the first—
Crowned—Crowing—on my Father's breast—
A half unconscious Queen—
But this time—Adequate—Erect,
With Will to choose, or to reject,
And I choose, just a Crown.
                                        —Emily Dickinson

Adrienne Rich has pointed out that this poem of Emily Dickinson's is a poem of great pride and self-confirmation, of transcending the patriarchal condition, of movement from unconsciousness to consciousness. She cautions us, however, not to give it a theological reading, because Emily Dickinson "used the Christian metaphor far more than she let it use her."[1]

I have quoted both Dickinson and Rich because they articulate at different levels the central challenge of a feminist biblical hermeneutics. Feminist consciousness radically throws into question all traditional religious names, texts, rituals, laws, and interpretative metaphors because they all bear "our Father's names." With Carol Christ[2] I would insist that the central spiritual and religious feminist quest is the quest for women's self-affirmation, survival, power, and self-determination.

Some of us have therefore argued that as self-identified women we cannot but leave behind patriarchal biblical religion and communities and create a new feminist religion on the boundaries of patriarchal religion and theology. Others claim biblical religion as an integral part of their own historical identity and religious experience. The Jewish feminist Alice Bloch articulates this claim well:

> I take pride in my Jewish heritage, and I am tired of hearing women dismiss Jewish identity as "oppressive" and "patriarchal." . . . Jewish identity is important to me, because being Jewish is an integral part of myself; it's my inheritance, my roots. Christian women sometimes have a hard time understanding this, because Christian identity is so much tied up with religious beliefs. It is possible to be an ex-Catholic or an ex-Baptist, but it is really not possible to be an ex-Jew.[3]

While agreeing with her insight that women's personal and religious self-identity is intertwined, I would maintain that Christian self-identity is not just tied up with religious beliefs but is also a communal-historical identity. Christian (and in my case Roman Catholic) feminists also do not relinquish their biblical roots and heritage. As the *ekklēsia* of women, we claim the center of Christian faith and community in a feminist process of transformation.

The Hermeneutical Center: Women-Church

The hermeneutical center of feminist biblical interpretation is the women-church *(ekklēsia gynaikōn)*, the movement of self-identified women and women-identified men in biblical religion. The *ekklēsia* of women is part of the wider women's movement in society and in religion that conceives itself not just as a civil rights movement but as a women's liberation movement. Its goal is not simply the "full humanity" of women, since humanity as we know it is male defined, but women's religious self-affirmation, power, and liberation from all patriarchal alienation, marginalization, and oppression. The Greek term *ekklēsia* means the public gathering of free citizens who assemble in order to determine their own and their children's communal well-being. It can be translated as the assembly, the synagogue, or the church of women. When as a Christian I use the expression women-church, I do not use it as an exclusionary[4] but as a political-oppositional term to patriarchy.

It thus becomes necessary to clarify here the way in which I use patriarchy as an explanatory concept. I do not define it in a general sense as a societal system in which men have power over women[5] but in the classical sense as it was defined in Aristotelian philosophy. Just as feminism is not just a worldview or perspective but a women's movement for change, so patriarchy is in my understanding not just ideological dualism or androcentric world construction in language but a social, economic, and political system of graded subjugations and oppressions. Therefore I do not speak simply about male oppressors and female oppressed, or see all men over and against all women. Patriarchy as a male pyramid specifies women's oppression in terms of the class, race, country, or religion of the men to whom they "belong."

Patriarchy as the basic descriptive model for feminist analysis allows us to conceptualize not only sexism but also racism and property-class relationships as basic structures of women's oppression. In a patriarchal society or religion, all women are bound into a system of male privilege and domination, but impoverished Third World women constitute the bottom of the oppressive patriarchal pyramid. Patriarchy cannot be toppled except when the women who form the bottom of the patriarchal pyramid, triply oppressed women, become liberated. All women's oppression and liberation is bound up with that of the colonialized and economically most exploited women. This was already recognized by one of the earliest statements of the radical women's liberation movement: "Until every woman is free, no woman is free."[6] "Equality from below" must become the liberative goal of women-church. In other words, as long as societal and religious patriarchy exists, women are not "liberated" and must struggle for survival and self-determination. Conversely, there is no one feminist theory, religion, or group that can claim to be fully liberated.

Since a critical analysis of patriarchy allows us to conceptualize the interaction of sexism, racism, classism, and militarist colonialism, such a feminist interpretation of liberation is not in its conception and goals white middle-class. All of us who are sufficiently educated to participate in a hermeneutical or theological discussion do not live our lives on the bottom of the patriarchal pyramid. Our experiences of oppression and marginalization are very different, but as women we all live in a society and culture that denies us our independence and self-determination.

My life and experience is quite different, for example, from that of my mother. In 1944, during street fighting, she had to leave her home with two small children and literally walk from Romania to a bombed-out Germany, surviving from day to day, begging for food, shelter, and clothing for her children. Nevertheless, my own struggles for survival as a woman in a clerical male profession have enabled me to understand more than my mother ever did what it means to be a woman in a patriarchal society. A feminist analysis of my own experience helps me realize that the baby given up for adoption could have been mine, the peasant girl in Guatemala without a childhood could be my daughter, the medieval woman burnt by the church as a witch could have been me, the senile woman left for days without food could be my future.

I have therefore argued that feminist theology must articulate its advocacy position not as an option for the oppressed but as the· self-identification of women in patriarchal society and religion, since all women are socialized to identify with men.[7] The more we identify as women and thereby overcome our patriarchal self-alienation, the more we will realize that the separation between white and black women, middle-class and poor women, native American and European women, Jewish and Christian women, Protestant and Catholic women, lesbian and heterosexual women, nun-women and lay-women is, in the words of Adrienne Rich, "a separation from ourselves."[8] Conversely, option for the most oppressed woman is an option for our women selves. Such an option allows us "to find God in ourselves" and to "love Her fiercely."[9]

The locus or place of divine revelation and grace is therefore not the Bible or the tradition of a patriarchal church but the *ekklēsia* of women and the lives of women who live the "option for our women selves." It is not simply "the experience" of women but the experience of women (and all those oppressed) struggling for liberation from patriarchal oppression [114].

> The dream of freedom for oneself in a world in which all women are free emerges from one's own life experience in which one is not free, precisely because one is a woman. The liberation of women is thus not an abstract goal . . . but is the motive for that process. Individual freedom and the freedom of all women are linked when one has reached the critical consciousness that we are united first in our unfreedom.[10]

The patriarchal dehumanization and victimization of triply oppressed women exhibits the full death-dealing powers of patriarchy, while their struggles for liberation and courage to survive is the fullest experience of God's grace in our midst. A feminist critical theology of liberation must therefore be particular and concrete. It must theologically explore women's particular experiences of marginalization, victimization, and oppression. At the same time it has to articulate our individual and historical experiences of liberation.

The God of Judith as well as the God of Jesus is Emmanuel, God with us in our struggles for liberation, freedom, and wholeness. The spiritual authority of women-church rests on this experience of grace in our midst.

Feminist biblical interpretation must therefore challenge the scriptural authority of patriarchal texts and explore how the Bible is used as a weapon against women in our struggles for liberation. It also must explore whether and how the Bible can become a resource in this struggle. A feminist biblical interpretation is thus first of all a political task. It remains mandatory because the Bible and its authority has been and is again today used as a weapon against women struggling for liberation.

From its inception, feminist interpretation and concern with scripture has been generated by the fact that the Bible was used to halt the emancipation of women and slaves. Not only in the last century but also today, the political Right laces its attacks against the feminist struggle for women's rights and freedoms in the political, economic, reproductive, intellectual, and religious spheres with biblical quotations and appeals to scriptural authority.[11] From countless pulpits and Sunday school classes, such patriarchal attacks are proclaimed as the "word of God." Anti-ERA groups, the cultural Total Woman movement, and the Moral Majority appeal to the teachings of the Bible on the American family and on creational differences between the sexes supposedly resulting in a different societal and ecclesial calling. At the same time, the political Right does not hesitate to quote the Bible against shelters for battered women, for physical punishment of children, against abortion even in cases of rape or child pregnancy, and against women's studies programs at state universities.[12]

At the same time the Bible has not served only to legitimate the oppression of white women, slaves, native Americans, Jews, and the poor. It has also provided authorization for women who rejected slavery, colonial exploitation, anti-Semitism, and misogynism as unbiblical and against God's will. It has inspired countless women to speak out against injustice, exploitation, and stereotyping and energized them to struggle against poverty, unfreedom, and denigration. The Guatemalan Indian and Christian revolutionary Rigoberta Menchu testifies to this:

> In the community we began to reflect together on what the Bible told us. The story of Judith, for example, impressed me very much: she beheaded the king to save her people. We too understood that faced with the violence of the rich, we have to respond with another kind of violence. The violence of justice.[13]

A Feminist Interpretive Model of Critical Evaluation

I propose elsewhere[14] that a feminist critical theology of liberation should develop a multidimensional model of biblical interpretation in order to assist women in their struggle for liberation. Such a model must be a feminist-critical and a historical-concrete model. It must not only show how individual biblical texts and writings functioned in their historical-political settings but also pay increased attention to the intersection and interplay of biblical texts with contemporary politics and socialization. It should not search for a feminist formalized principle, a universal perspective, or a historical liberating dynamics but should carefully analyze how the Bible functions concretely in women's struggle for survival. Key elements in such a model, as far as I can see, are the following: (1) suspicion rather than acceptance of biblical authority, (2) critical evaluation rather than correlation, (3) interpretation through proclamation, (4) remembrance and historical reconstruction, and (5) interpretation through celebration and ritual.

First: A feminist Christian apologetics presumes that we can trust our lives to the "word of God" in the Bible and that we should submit to its authority and liberating power. It therefore insists that a hermeneutics of suspicion should only be applied to the history of exegesis and contemporary interpretations. While a liberation-theological interpretation affirms the liberating dynamics of the biblical texts, a feminist critical hermeneutics of suspicion places a warning label on all biblical texts: *Caution! Could be dangerous to your health and survival.* Not only is scripture interpreted by a long line of men and proclaimed in patriarchal churches, it is also authored by men, written in androcentric language, reflective of religious male experience, selected and transmitted by male religious leadership. Without question, the Bible is a male book. If Mary Daly is right that here also "the medium is the message," self-identified women struggling for survival should avoid it like the plague. The first and never-ending task of a hermeneutics of suspicion, therefore, is to elaborate as much as possible the patriarchal, destructive aspects and oppressive elements in the Bible. Such an interpretation must uncover not only sexist biblical language but also the oppressive language of racism, anti-Judaism, exploitation, colonialism, and militarism. An interpretation of suspicion must name the language of hate by its true name and not mystify it or explain it away.

Yet women in all walks of life testify to a different, inspiring, challenging, and liberating experience with the Bible. If we cannot write off all women who find meaning in scripture as unliberated and unfeminist, we have to use a hermeneutics of suspicion to detect the antipatriarchal elements and functions of biblical texts, which are obscured and made invisible by androcentric language and concepts. Moreover, we have to acknowledge that not all biblical stories, traditions, and texts reflect the experience of men in power or were written in order to legitimate the patriarchal status quo.

Second: If the *ekklēsia* of women has the authority "to choose and to reject" biblical texts, we have to develop a theological interpretive principle for feminist critical evaluation rather than an interpretive principle and method of correlation. Such an interpretation must sort through particular biblical texts and test out in a process of critical analysis and evaluation how much their content and function perpetrates and legitimates patriarchal structures, not only in their original historical contexts but also in our contemporary situation. Conversely, all biblical texts must be tested as to their feminist liberating content and function in their historical and contemporary contexts. Such a feminist hermeneutics of critical evaluation has to articulate criteria and principles for evaluating particular texts, biblical books, traditions, or interpretations. Such criteria or principles must be derived from a systematic exploration of women's experience of oppression and liberation.

Because of the importance of specific feminist analyses and critical evaluations, I have argued that a feminist interpretation ought not to reduce the richness of biblical texts and traditions to one particular text or tradition, as the neoorthodox "canon within the canon" model does. It also should not separate form and content and then formalize and universalize them to a principle or dynamic, as the method of critical correlation (Schillebeeckx, Tracy) or confrontation (Küng) does.[15] Although Tillich had criticized Barth's dialectical method, his "neo-dialectical method of correlation" is still motivated by the apologetic intent that engages in a critical dialogue of "yes and no" between contemporary culture and biblical religion in order to end with an affirmative "yes" to religion. Such a method of correlation, however, rests on "the distinction between the unchanging content of the Christian message and the changing forms of cultural expression."[16]

A feminist method of correlation adopts the same distinction insofar as it separates the sociocritical prophetic-messianic principle or dynamics from its concrete historical articulations and deformations on the one hand and formalizes feminist experience and analysis on the other, in such a way that it becomes a critical principle of "affirmation and promotion of the full humanity of women." It does so in order to correlate both the prophetic-biblical and the feminist critical principles with each other. As Rosemary Ruether has said in chapter 9:

> The Bible can be appropriated as a source of liberating paradigms only if it can be seen that there is a correlation between the feminist critical principle and that critical principle by which biblical thought critiques itself and renews its vision as the authentic Word of God over against corrupting and sinful deformations. It is my contention here that there is such a correlation between biblical and feminist critical principles [117].

As alternative option I have proposed that biblical feminists need not presume such a correlation or configuration, but nevertheless in a process of critical evaluation we are able to find some liberating paradigms and resources in biblical texts. This is the case not because a correlation between feminist and biblical critical principles can be presupposed but because the historical experience of women-church with the Bible allows us to do so. Yet in order to find feminist biblical resources, we have first to bring to bear the full force of the feminist critique upon biblical texts and religion.

Third: Since today, as in the past, the political Right fights its "holy war" against feminism under the banner of the doctrinal paradigm of biblical interpretation, our defense must directly address the question of the Word of God as proclaimed in scripture.[17] We have therefore to develop a hermeneutics of proclamation that undercuts the authority claims of patriarchal scriptural texts. As I have already suggested in my contribution to *The Liberating Word,* feminist theology must first of all denounce all texts and traditions that perpetrate and legitimate oppressive patriarchal structures and ideologies. We no longer should proclaim them as the "word of God" for contemporary communities and people if we do not want to turn God into a God of oppression.

A careful feminist assessment of the selection and reception of biblical texts for proclamation in the liturgy must therefore precede an inclusive translation of them. Patriarchal texts should not be allowed to remain in the lectionary but should be replaced by texts affirming the discipleship of equals. An "inclusive translation" can only be made of those lectionary texts which, in a critical feminist process of evaluation, are identified as articulating a liberating vision for women struggling for self-affirmation and wholeness, lest we are in danger of covering up the patriarchal character of the Bible [12, 13, 107].

Such a hermeneutics of proclamation also must assess the contemporary political context and psychological function of biblical interpretations and texts. It must explore how even feminist-neutral or feminist-positive biblical texts can have an oppressive impact on the lives of contemporary women, if they are used in order to inculcate misogynist attitudes and patriarchal behavior. For instance, in our culture, in which women, primarily, are socialized into sacrificing love and self-abnegation, the biblical commandment of love and the proclamation of the cross can be culturally misused to sustain voluntary service and the acceptance of sexual violence. In exploring the interaction between biblical texts and societal feminine values and behavior, we also have to pay attention to its religious contexts. As Susan Thistlethwaite has pointed out in chapter 6, biblical texts have a different meaning and authority for battered women rooted in different ecclesial communities [99]. Much more work needs to be done on the intersection of the Bible with contemporary culture, politics, and society.

Fourth: Such a hermeneutics of proclamation must be balanced by a hermeneutics of remembrance, which recovers *all* biblical traditions and texts through a feminist historical reconstruction. Feminist meaning is not only derived from the egalitarian-feminist surplus of androcentric texts but is also to be found in and through androcentric texts and patriarchal history. Rather than abandon the memory of our foresisters' sufferings, visions, and hopes in our patriarchal biblical past, such a hermeneutics reclaims their sufferings, struggles, and victories through the subversive power of the "remembered" past. Rather than relinquish patriarchal biblical traditions, a hermeneutics of remembrance seeks to develop a feminist critical method and historical model for moving beyond the androcentric text to the history of women in biblical religion.

Such an interpretation recognizes methodologically that androcentric language as generic conventional language makes women invisible by subsuming us under linguistic masculine terms. It mentions women only when we are exceptional or cause problems. To take androcentric biblical texts as reflecting reality does not recognize the ideological, obfuscating character of androcentric language. To reconstruct women's participation in biblical history, we therefore have to read the "women passages" as indicators and clues that women were at the center of biblical life. In other words, if we take the conventional ideological character of androcentric language seriously, we can claim that women were leaders and full members in biblical religion until proven otherwise. The burden of historical proof is shifted when we read texts that speak about the leadership and presence of women, or those that are injunctions to proper "feminine" behavior, not as descriptive and comprehensive information but as the visible tip of an iceberg which for the most part is submerged.

An interpretation through remembrance must articulate theoretical models that can place women not on the periphery but at the center of biblical community and history. In my book *In Memory of Her,* I have proposed patriarchy as such a social-historical model for reconstructing early Christian origins in a feminist perspective. While feminist theology usually utilizes androcentric dualism as its basic exploratory concept for feminist analysis and reconstruction, I propose that we use patriarchy as articulated in Aristotelian philosophy as a basic explanatory concept for the reconstruction of women's history in Western society in general and in Christian history in particular.

Androcentric dualism must then be understood as ideological justification of patriarchal structures. It is articulated whenever non-patriarchal, egalitarian societal or religious possibilities exist or are at least thinkable. This was the case in Athenian democracy, where it became necessary to claim "different natures" for freeborn women and slave women as well as men because of the democratic notion of citizenship. Similarly, in early Christianity, misogynist texts and patriarchal injunctions were generated because the discipleship of equals stood in tension with Greco-Roman patriarchal structures. The gradual patriarchalization of the church in the second and third centuries not only engendered the exclusion of all women from ecclesial leadership but also eliminated the freedoms that slave women had gained by joining the Christian movement.

Insofar as androcentric biblical texts are generated by the tension between patriarchal societal and ecclesial structures and the vision and praxis of the discipleship of equals, they allow us still a glimpse of women's engagement and leadership in the early Christian movement. Although the scriptural canon preserves only remnants of the nonpatriarchal early Christian ethos, these remnants allow us still to recognize that patriarchal structures are not inherent to Christian community, although they have become historically dominant. Therefore a feminist hermeneutics of remembrance can reclaim early Christian history as our own history and religious vision. Women-church has a long history and tradition, which can claim the discipleship of equals as its scriptural roots. In sum, a feminist hermeneutics of remembrance has to keep alive the memory of patriarchal biblical oppression as well as the memory of the struggles and victories of biblical women who acted in the power of the Spirit.

Fifth: Interpretation through remembrance and historical reconstruction must be supplemented by a hermeneutics of creative ritualization. Such an interpretation allows women-church to enter the biblical story with the help of historical imagination, artistic recreation, and liturgical celebration. A method of creative actualization seeks to retell biblical stories from a feminist perspective, to reformulate biblical visions and injunctions in the perspective of the discipleship of equals, and to create narrative amplifications of the feminist remnants that have survived in biblical texts. In such a process of creative revisioning, women-church can utilize all available means of artistic imagination, literary creativity, music, and dance.

In legend and apocryphal writings, in liturgy and sacred hymns, in feast days and liturgical cycles, the patriarchal church has ritualized certain aspects and texts of the Bible as well as celebrated the "founding fathers" of biblical religion. A feminist interpretation of creative ritualization reclaims for women-church the same imaginative freedoms, popular creativity, and liturgical powers. Women not only rewrite biblical stories but also reformulate patriarchal prayers and create feminist rituals for celebrating our foremothers. We rediscover in story and poetry, in drama and dance, in song and liturgy our biblical foresisters' sufferings and victories. In ever-new images and symbols, feminist liturgies seek to rename the God of the Bible and the biblical vision. We sing litanies of praise to our foresisters and pray laments of mourning for the wasted lives of our foremothers. Only by reclaiming our religious imagination and our ritual powers of naming can women-church dream new dreams and see new visions. We do so, however, in the full awareness that such creative feminist participation in the biblical story and history must be won in and through a critical process of evaluation.

In conclusion, what leads us to perceive biblical texts as providing resources in the struggle for liberation from patriarchal oppression, as well as models for the transformation of the patriarchal church, is not some special canon of texts that can claim divine authority. Rather, it is the experience of women themselves in their struggles for liberation. I have therefore suggested that we understand the Bible as a structuring prototype of women-church rather than as a definite archetype; as an open-ended paradigm that sets experiences in motion and invites transformations. Rather than reduce its pluriformity and richness to abstract principle or ontological immutable archetype to be applied to and repeated in ever-new situations, I suggest the notion of historical prototype open to its own transformation.

Such an understanding of the Bible as formative prototype allows us to explore models and traditions of liberating praxis as well as of patriarchal repression. It allows us to reclaim the whole Bible not as normative but as an experiential enabling authority, as the legacy and heritage of women-church. Such a notion of the Bible not as a mythic archetype but as a historical prototype provides women-church with a sense of its own ongoing history as well as Christian identity. It is able to acknowledge the dynamic process of biblical resources, challenges, and new visions under the changing conditions of the church's cultural-historical situations.

In and through structural and creative transformation, the Bible can become holy scripture for women-church. Insofar as the interpretive model proposed here does not identify biblical revelation with androcentric texts and patriarchal structures, it maintains that such revelation and inspiration is found among the discipleship community of equals in the past and the present. Insofar as the model proposed here locates revelation not in biblical texts but in the experience of women struggling for liberation from patriarchy, it requires that a feminist critical hermeneutics of liberation read and actualize the Bible in the context of believing communities of women, in the context of women-church.

II

Authority and the Challenge of Feminist Interpretation

Letty M. Russell

Feminists of the Jewish and Christian faiths are faced with a basic dilemma. Are they to be faithful to the teachings of the Hebrew scriptures and the Christian scriptures, or are they to be faithful to their own integrity as whole human beings? This dilemma is underlined by Margaret Farley in her analysis of feminist consciousness [49]. It surfaces in Katharine Sakenfeld's description of feminist uses of biblical materials [64]. Rosemary Ruether's proposal for a feminist principle as "the affirmation of and promotion of the full humanity of women" again underlines this dilemma [115]. In fact, authority is a theme that surfaces constantly in this book, either by the intention of the authors or by the reactions of their readers!

Whether or not feminists choose to discuss this issue, it is pressed upon them every time they propose an interpretation or perspective that challenges a dominant view of scriptural authority and interpretation. Among those who consider the Bible to be literally the Word of God, efforts to provide more inclusive translation and interpretation of texts evoke anger and fear of losing the ground of faith. Among those who consider historical critical scholarship as the norm for what is to be accepted in biblical interpretation, feminist interpretations are considered biased and unfounded and dismissed with little self-examination of white male academic bias. Even among the contributors to this volume, there is a great deal of disagreement about the particular mix of religious tradition, experience, and academic research that leads to feminist critical principles.

In this chapter I would like to take up this question of biblical authority. I will begin from the perspective of my own life experience as a Christian, white, middle-class, Protestant woman in inner-city ministry. Questions of authority are ultimately understood in terms of our own religious, social, political, and economic setting or context. It is important to make that context clear and invite others to share their own contexts and how these shape their views of authority. Readers who have missed this connection in their own lives may have explored the influence of history on feminist consciousness with Barbara Zikmund in chapter 1 or seen the impact of context in Katie Cannon's description of the way biblical interpretation in the Black church "dealt with contingencies in the real-lived context" [21, 38]. After discussing the biblical basis of my theology, I want to examine here what it means to speak of the Bible as authoritative and then suggest how a feminist paradigm of authority might help to address the dilemma of the "hit parade of authority."

The Biblical Basis of My Theology

In spite of the patriarchal nature of the biblical texts, I myself have no intention of giving up the biblical basis of my theology. With Rosemary Ruether I would argue that the Bible has a critical or liberating tradition embodied in its "prophetic-messianic" message of continuing self-critique [116–117]. The evidence for a biblical message of liberation for women, as for other marginalized groups, is not found just in particular stories about women or particular female images of God. It is found in God's intention for the mending of all creation. The Bible has authority in my life because it makes sense of my experience and speaks to me about the meaning and purpose of my humanity in Jesus Christ. In spite of its ancient and patriarchal worldviews, in spite of its inconsistencies and mixed messages, the story of God's love affair with the world leads me to a vision of New Creation that impels my life.

Scripture and Script

I am one of those for whom the Bible continues to be a liberating word as I hear it together with others and struggle to live out its story. For me the Bible is "scripture," or sacred writing, because it functions as "script," or prompting for life. Its authority in my life stems from its story of God's invitation to participation in the restoration of wholeness, peace, and justice in the world. Responding to this invitation has made it my own story, or script, through the power of the Spirit at work in communities of struggle and faith. In the same way I could say with Elisabeth Fiorenza that the Bible provides a "prototype" for my own story that "sets experiences in motion and invites transformation" [135].

My particular story is one shaped by seventeen years with a poor, racially mixed community of struggle and witness in the East Harlem Protestant Parish in New York City. In such a context the Bible did not have all the answers, but it provided a source of meaning and hope for our lives. Somehow the texts we really lived with, and struggled with, seemed to speak in ever new ways on our road toward freedom. In East Harlem the story of God's concern for humanity showed us that "nobodies" in the eyes of the dominant society could be "somebodies." I still believe this, believe that in God's sight I am not marginal but that, like my Black and Hispanic sisters and brothers in East Harlem, I came created by God and called by the biblical word of promise to become what God intends me to become: a partner in the mending of creation.

Mending Creation

The particular interpretive key that assists me in continuing to give assent is the witness of scripture to God's promise (for the mending of creation) on its way to fulfillment. That which denies this intention of God for the liberation of groaning creation in all its parts does not compel or evoke my assent (i.e., it is not authoritative). Although I arrived at this interpretive key through my own life story, it is not unlike the interpretive key proposed by Ruether as God's affirmation of the full humanity of women and all persons seen in the prophetic witness of scripture against injustice and dehumanization. Nor is it very dissimilar to Fiorenza's interpretive key of Jesus and the discipleship of equals, even though she arrives at the key through a very different process of careful biblical reconstruction in her book *In Memory of Her.* [1]

As a feminist I look to the horizon of expectation of the Bible as the source of my own expectation of justice and liberation. In this way the Bible is not only prototype, it is also "a memory of the future" that constantly opens up the possibility of new life through the small glimpses and anticipations of God's partnership at work in the biblical story and in our own lives. In God's action of New Creation, women and men are already set free to develop new ways of relating to one another, to the world, and to God. This freedom of living in the "already, but not yet" of the New Creation is key to those who are struggling with structures of oppression and with biblical texts that are used to justify and even to bless these structures in ways such as those described by Susan Thistlethwaite in chapter 8 on the oppressive (or liberating) role of scripture in the lives of battered women [99]. We are not left with stories of the past in the biblical witness. The stories themselves are open-ended. There is *more to come.* And this anticipation of New Creation can be the source of actions to bring this vision of new life into the present struggles for human dignity.[2]

Perhaps it would seem more useful to give up on the Bible as a normative source of my theology, but I don't seem to be able to do that. The biblical witness continues to evoke my consent, even as I reject many of its teachings as well as its patriarchal context. And, as Mary Ann Tolbert has pointed out in her article in *The Bible and Feminist Hermeneutics,* I am not alone in this. She claims that feminist biblical scholarship is profoundly paradoxical because "one must struggle against God as enemy assisted by God as helper, or one must defeat the Bible as patriarchal authority by using the Bible as liberator."[3] I continue to live with this paradox because the Bible still helps to make sense of who I am, and because the biblical witness opens the way to a future that will be so radically different from the present that it will be called *new!* (Rom. 8:31–32).

Authoritative Use of Scripture

The issue of authority is not an easy one, for it is basic to the way we see and interpret the world in which we live. As Sallie McFague has shown in her book *Metaphorical Theology,* paradigms or interpretive frameworks for understanding reality provide total contexts for interpretation or meaning and are very slow to change.[4] Each time there is a paradigm shift in the field of theology, much of the prior theological understanding continues, yet there is a new understanding of that which evokes consent of faith and action. Each theological shift involves a change in what counts as authoritative in the tradition. Feminist theologies, in articulating such a paradigm shift, bring into question what has been understood as authoritative in every aspect of biblical religion, including the use of scripture in academic and faith communities.

Interpretive Framework

The discussions of feminist interpretation among those who helped shape this volume of essays seemed to move to a consensus that the authority of the Bible has to be understood in a way that accounts for the fact that, frequently, the texts are not only contradictory but also sexist, racist, and triumphalist. No interpretation of authority that reinforces patriarchal structures of domination would be acceptable for feminist interpretation. The Bible is understood to be a "dangerous book" that has often been used to teach slaves and women to be subservient to masters and to provide God's blessing for warfare. It is not surprising to note that some Black Christians refuse to read sections of Paul's letters in church,[5] or that some women have added the subtitle, *This book may be dangerous to your health.* We know that everything the Bible says is not equally helpful to us as women of faith and that there are false interpretations and misuses of the scriptures. The Bible is especially dangerous if we call it "the Word of God" and think that divine inspiration means that everything we read is right.[6] But divine inspiration means that God's Spirit has the power to make the story speak to us from faith to faith. The Bible is accepted as the Word of God when communities of faith understand God to be speaking to them in and through its message.

How does the Bible come to make sense in communities of faith? Not through a literal reading of the text but through what David Kelsey calls an "imaginative construal" or configuration of criteria that evoke our consent and become normative for the way we would live the life of faith.

> To say that the Biblical texts taken as scripture are "authority" for the church and theology is to say that they provide patterns determinate enough to *function* as basis for assessment of the Christian aptness of current churchly forms of life and speech and of theologians' proposals for reform of that life and speech.[7]

The particular pattern of criteria is an imaginative judgment concerning the use of scripture and the mode in which God is understood as present among the faithful [59].

According to Kelsey, the imaginative act of the theologian in creating a configuration of criteria that evoke consent is accountable to the common life of the religious community out of which she or he speaks. He lists three limits of theological imagination or claim to authoritative use of scripture: The claim must include intelligible discourse capable of consistent formulation and reasoned elaboration and justification; it must reflect the structure of tradition as scripture is used to nurture and reform the identity of a particular faith community; and it must be seriously imaginable in the particular cultural context where the interpretation takes place.[8] Kelsey's functional view of what it means that the Bible has authority in any given interpretation seems to be at least one way of recognizing the variety of approaches to authority that are present among feminists interpreting scripture. His concept of "imaginative construal" comes very close to what McFague and others have called an interpretive framework or paradigm: a common perspective on reality made up of a particular constellation of beliefs, values, and methods.[9] In addition, it seems to me that the suggested limits of interpretation point to a way that feminist and liberation critical perspective are beginning to shift the prevailing interpretive paradigms.

Feminist Interpretation

The imaginative configuration of feminist interpretation seeks to be a form of intelligible discourse, speaking in a logical, consistent, and documented way out of a variety of academic disciplines and religious traditions. Yet along with other liberation theologies, stress is placed on an inductive process of action and reflection in which a major criterion for consistency is the way that reflection is brought together with action. As we can see in Fiorenza's chapter, the method of interpretation is integrated with actions of advocacy [131].

Feminist interpretation most certainly makes use of the structure of tradition, but it raises radical questions about the oppressive ways that scripture and tradition have been used and about the unfaithfulness of church and synagogue as guardians of that tradition. An excellent example of the reconstruction of theological tradition is found in Rosemary Ruether's *Sexism and God Talk.* Here she takes up traditional subjects of Christian theology, such as God, Christ, the Spirit, and the Church, and not only critiques the previous sexist formulations but provides clues for reformulating Christian theology.

The third limit on imaginative configuration, speaking of what is *seriously imaginable,* has been transformed from a limit to a fundamental norm in feminist interpretation. As Margaret Farley has pointed out, speaking of what is seriously imaginable in the lives of women and other oppressed groups raises questions of whether a God who is sexist, racist, or classist is God at all.[10] This interpretation cannot imagine a God who does not seek to be partner with all humankind in the mending of creation. It therefore looks at the Bible from the perspective of women struggling for this human wholeness and finds many and unexpected echoes in stories of women, such as those presented by Sharon Ringe, Cheryl Exum, and Drorah Setel in this volume.[11]

Perhaps the most important limit on feminist imaginative configuration of scriptural authority is the community of struggle, or what Fiorenza calls "women-church" [126]. In this interpretation, communities of oppression, where women and men are struggling for equality and mutuality, become prisms through which God's action in the mending of creation is to be understood. Theological imagination exercised apart from this prophetic voice is no longer to be considered "seriously imaginable." Along with liberation theologies, feminist theologies have thus signaled the beginning of a paradigm shift. This is what Sallie McFague has called a "theological revolution," and it includes a transformation of the meaning of authority.[12]

A Feminist Paradigm of Authority

The feminist paradigm of authority is a shift in interpretive framework that affects all the authority structures in religion and society, including the claim that scripture evokes our consent to faith and action. The prevailing paradigm of authority in Christian and Jewish religion is one of authority as domination. In this framework, all questions of authority are settled with reference to the "hit parade of authority." But, as the feminist-liberation paradigm of authority in community begins to become the one most "seriously imaginable" to women and men of faith, a new framework emerges that allows for multiple authorities to enrich, rather than to outrank, one another.

Shift in Paradigm

The paradigm that no longer makes sense to feminists is that of *authority as domination*. This constellation of beliefs, values, and methods shared as a common perspective tends to predominate in church and university and in most theological research and dialogue.[13] Consciously or unconsciously, reality is seen in the form of a hierarchy, or pyramid. Ordination and every other topic are viewed in terms of super—and sub—ordination. Things are assigned a divine order, with God at the top, men next, and so on down to dogs, plants, and "impersonal" nature. This paradigm reinforces ideas of authority *over* community and refuses to admit the ideas and persons that do not (wish to) fit into the established hierarchies of thought or social structures.

In this framework, theological "truth" is sought through ordering the hierarchy of doctrines, orders, and degrees. The difficulty for women and Third World groups is that their perspectives often do not fit in the pyramid structure of such a system of interpretation. The price of inclusion in the theological enterprise is loss of their own perspective and culture in order to do "good theology" as defined by "those at the top." Those who persist in raising questions and in affirming perspectives that do not fit in the paradigm pay the price of further marginalization. The extreme form of this is the emergence of "heretical groups" that are forced out of the theological conversation and thus lose the possibility of mutual development and critique.

This paradigm of reality is an inadequate theological perspective because it provides a religious rationale for the domination and oppression of the weak by the oppressive political, economic, and religious power elites. Such a view is clearly contrary to the prophetic-messianic promise of God's welcome to all the outsiders (Luke 4:16–30). It is also an inadequate paradigm of authority in a world so diverse that it no longer makes sense to try to fit people into such a rigid view of theological and social truth. Lastly, it discourages cooperation in the search for meaning because it frames discussion as a competition of ideas in which all participants aim at gaining the top spot and vanquishing the others.

The emerging feminist paradigm trying to make sense of biblical and theological truth claims is that of *authority as partnership.* In this view, reality is interpreted in the form of a circle of interdependence. Ordering is explored through inclusion of diversity in a rainbow spectrum that does not require that persons submit to the "top" but, rather, that they participate in the common task of creating an interdependent community of humanity and nature. Authority is exercised *in* community and tends to reinforce ideas of cooperation, with contributions from a wide diversity of persons enriching the whole. When difference is valued and respected, those who have found themselves marginal to church or society begin to discover their own worth as human beings.

This paradigm of reality is not just a romantic dream; many persons, including feminists, are trying to act out of this perspective. In fact, it is the most realistic alternative possible in a world bent on self-destruction so that some nation or group may claim "victory." Authority as partnership also begins to provide a theological perspective that seeks to discover a more inclusive consensus on theological issues. This is, perhaps, not unlike the meaning of consensus in the early Christian community, which was a consensus in the shared story of God's love in Jesus Christ rather than doctrinal consensus (Phil. 2:1–2). It no longer tries to get all persons to accept one neat priority system of theological truth but, rather, welcomes all who are willing to share in building a community of human wholeness that is inclusive of women and men. Very importantly, from the perspective of feminist interpretation, authority as partnership frames discussion in terms of communal search and sharing in which all can rejoice when anyone gains a new insight that can be shared together on the journey toward the New Creation. It is this theoretical framework that provides a new way of approaching issues of biblical authority.

A New Framework

This new framework is particularly important in the ongoing discussion of whether the interpretive key for feminists should be located within the biblical canonical tradition or outside of that tradition. Elisabeth Fiorenza has argued that the authority to evoke consent should come from "the experience of women (and all those oppressed) struggling for liberation from patriarchal oppression" [128]. She rejects the correlation of a biblical critical principle with a feminist critical principle that is key to both Rosemary Ruether's and my own understanding of biblical authority [131].

Fiorenza's position is very important, as she calls for a critical perspective that is based in the concrete life experience of women, expressed in the political task of advocacy and liberating praxis [128]. Fiorenza is no longer willing to play the authority game, submitting feminist norms to "higher" biblical authority and androcentric perceptions.[14] The canon and the rules about authority that come out of a patriarchal mind-set of domination must not decide the basis for feminist interpretation. Yet in the community paradigm of authority, it is no longer necessary to argue that one feminist principle must exclude or dominate another in "hit parade" fashion. All our insights come out of our particular life experience and expertise. For this reason, Ruether and I are far more likely to appeal to theological principles of interpretation than to historical critical reconstruction, because we are theologians, not New Testament scholars. But we share a common commitment to a feminist paradigm rooted in advocacy for women as the oppressed of every oppressed group.

In any case, authority exercised *in* community makes it possible for all of us to stand together in our search for critical principles of feminist interpretation. In this view there can be no one archetype of unchanging basis of authority. Like the power of God's love, authority as partnership does not coerce people into consent. The issue is no longer to be understood as a competition between feminist critical principles drawn from within and from outside of the canon [118–119]. Rather, the issue is how stories and actions of faithfulness can help us to celebrate and live out signs of God's justice and shalom for all humanity. As prototype, the Bible is not a captive of any one group or principle [135]. Experience, tradition, biblical witness, and intellectual research enrich each other in a rainbow of ordered (but not subordinated) diversity, in a synergetic perspective of authority in community.

When we take this shift in the paradigm of authority as a starting point for understanding the clues for feminist interpretation, we are moving toward what Bruce Birch has called "a de-absolutized canon which allows for the honoring of ancient witness to the degree that it reveals to us the basic truths of our faith, while at the same time honoring the power and authority of our own experience of God."[15] In the perspective of authority in community, the interpretive key is no longer one external or one internal biblical key but rather a configuration of sources of faith that seek to enrich the way God might be present with us.

The shift in feminist interpretive framework means that we no longer need to divide feminist experience and biblical witness. As Susan Thistlethwaite says in chapter 8, feminist method emerges as "a process of interrogation between text and experience" that "proceeds over time" [98]. The two belong together, as communities of struggle and faith in every age respond to the invitation to partnership with God in the mending of creation and discover that their lives and their understanding of the biblical witness have been changed.

In the light of this understanding of authority as partnership, it is no longer necessary to accept the dilemma of choice between faithfulness to the teaching of scripture or to our own integrity as human beings. For in a rainbow spectrum of faithful witness there will never be the possibility of such a choice. In the midst of shared feminist community, some will stress one thing and some another. But together we will continue to find our way through the thickets of patriarchal ideas and structures that challenge us to abandon the "hope that is in" us (1 Peter 3:15) for which we seek to give account.

Postscript:
Jottings on the Journey

Phyllis Trible

Many voices and many visions fill this volume. They belong to feminists who search the scriptures and do not always find in them eternal life. These women also scrutinize the traditional keepers of scripture and do find in them perpetual patriarchy. Suspicion thus joins commitment in this journey to discover a biblical faith that yields wholeness and well-being.

With so serious an agenda, it is no wonder that now and then the voices strain, crack, and break; that sharp differences emerge, not to be resolved; that at times the visions appear through a glass darkly. Yet a certain tenacity prevails. Refusing to let go without a blessing, the women call the Bible and its interpreters to account-ability. The just persistence of their cause impresses itself upon the reader to evoke innumerable theological reflections. A few of these become jottings in the postscript of a traveling companion.

Liberating the Bible from patriarchy is the first theological con-sideration. It applies a time-honored principle to a contemporary issue. From the ancient world to the present, lovers of scripture have released it from the prison of the past to speak to the living. The discipline of tradition history demonstrates this procedure in the Bible itself. Theologians of ancient Israel and the early church reinterpreted texts in light of subsequent events. Such activity freed the scriptures to give and take new meanings. Later generations continued the process. Translators redeemed the Bible from for-eign tongues and alien idioms. Faced with intellectual challenges, the church fathers used allegorical exegesis to save scripture from obscurantism.[1] Similarly, their medieval successors sought to eman-cipate the text for the Christian life. With the Reformers came a decisive use of the principle. They delivered the Bible from ecclesiastical control. On the current scene, the hermeneutic operates among scholars who explore the ancient Near Eastern context of the Hebrew scriptures or the Jewish and Hellenistic roots of the New Testament. They liberate the Bible from incompleteness and provincialism. Other commentators save it from scholarly captivity to nourish the poor, the outcast, and the oppressed.[2]

In whatever ways it develops, the liberation of scripture marks interpretation old and new. By using the principle, feminists stand within a long history; by applying it to the issue of idolatrous patriarchy, they introduce a radically new subject.[3] From this history they draw comfort, caution, and courage. With this subject they lay the prophetic ax to the root of the tree. Grounded in a paradigm of domination and subordination, patriarchy does not bear good fruit.

The traditional guardians of the scriptural forest protest. They say that the preserve cannot be altered; it must be maintained intact. "Scripture is fixed; you must not change the text. You cannot make it say what it does not say." This apodictic protest initiates a second theological reflection: A fixed, unchangeable text is neither possible nor desirable. For better or worse, be it conscious or unconscious, the text is always being changed. Although translators and interpreters readily acknowledge this truth at some levels, they resist its validity at others. Nevertheless, theological warrant for changing the text lies at the heart of scripture and faith—the name of the Holy One. In postexilic times Jews ceased to utter the sacred name Yahweh for fear of profanation. They made substitutions, chief among them the Hebrew word *Adonai*, meaning "Lord." While they retained the original name YHWH in script, they removed it from speech. As a substitute, not a synonym, for Yahweh, the title *Adonai* inevitably altered the meaning of the text.[4] Throughout centuries Christians have joined Jews in honoring this deliberate change.

This datum is pertinent to current discussion on sexist language and the Bible. History shows that theological warrant for changing the text exists within believing communities. Intentionally, people of faith have altered language to give meaning different from the original, and yet in the process they have neither destroyed nor removed the evidence. On the issue of translation, feminists and others may find in this precedent an ancient helper fit for a contemporary task.[5]

A third jotting focuses on the canon. In the past, the concept of a canon within the canon has delineated an authoritative core in scripture to which the rest is subordinate. A theology of the mighty acts of God based on the exodus event illustrates the concept. Traditions that do not reflect this stance, like the wisdom literature, are deemed less valuable. Such a theological center orders and controls meaning, it minimizes richness and diversity, and it absolutizes certain texts at the expense of others. Feminists are not alone in rejecting this view of the canon as traditionally formulated.[6]

Yet in a pluralized and flexible form, the principle is apt for understanding feminist perspectives set forth in this volume. Repeatedly, the writers employ canons within the canon. They use sections of scripture (as well as external values) to judge other sections. For some feminists, such as Rosemary Ruether, the prophetic-messianic tradition constitutes the authoritative core. The rest of the canon is subjected to its criticism even as its limitations are exposed by different social and temporal settings. Other feminists—Elisabeth Schüssler Fiorenza, for example—establish a comparable, yet distinct, canon with the claim that only the nonsexist and nonandrocentric traditions of the Bible have revelatory power. Again, as for Katie Cannon, the Bible "in essence," but not *in toto,* is "the highest source of authority for most Black women." They identify with passages and themes that speak life; they reject those that bid death. A principle of selectivity is also present in the separation of descriptive and culturally conditioned texts from prescriptive and existentially valid ones. With such readings, feminists employ canons within the canon. Like many other interpreters, they use scripture to judge and correct scripture for appropriation in their lives.[7] In turn, the Bible, if allowed, provides feminism with a needed critique of itself. This thought is the final jotting on the journey.

Prophetic movements are not exempt from sin. Even as feminism announces judgment on patriarchy and calls for repentance and change, it needs ever to be aware of its own potential for idolatry. No document teaches this lesson better than scripture.

Liberating the Bible, changing the text, using scripture to evaluate scripture, allowing the Bible to exercise a prophetic critique—reflections on these themes show continuities between feminist interpretation and traditional hermeneutics; the content of the themes yields the discontinuities. If the former offer a common ground from which to work, the latter require a transformation in the land. Thus the jottings hint at the contributions of this volume to an ongoing discussion among feminism, scripture, and interpreters. Many voices and many visions seek a biblical faith that brings wholeness and well-being. What, then, comes next? More work in exegesis and in the historical and social milieu of scripture[8]; the expansion of the enterprise to welcome other women and men; and, perhaps, in God's good time, a biblical theology of womanhood.

Notes

Introduction: Liberating the Word

1. Russell, *The Liberating Word*, pp. 14–15. The complete reference for this title, and others similarly shortened, may be found listed under Additional Resources.

2. Numbers in brackets refer to pages in this volume.

3. See Additional Resources for these works and for other references to feminist interpretation.

4. *An Inclusive-Language Lectionary: Readings for Year B* (1984), pp. 183–185, 186. See also *Readings for Year A* (1983).

5. *Journal for the Study of the Old Testament* (hereafter referred to as *JSOT*) 22:3–71 (February 1982).

6. Dorothy C. Bass, "Women's Studies and Biblical Studies: An Historical Perspective," *JSOT* 22:10–11. See also Elizabeth Cady Stanton, *The Woman's Bible*.

7. Katharine Doob Sakenfeld, "Response to Rosemary Radford Ruether's 'Christology and Feminism: Can a Male Savior Help Women?' " April 1981, unpublished; now revised as chapter 4.

8. Phyllis Trible, "Feminist Hermeneutics and Biblical Studies," *The Christian Century*, February 1982, pp. 116–118.

9. Bruce Birch and Gibson Winter in discussion of the Biblical Liberation Hermeneutic Project, December 20, 1982, New York City. Cf. Birch, "Response to Elisabeth Schüssler Fiorenza . . . ," Feminist Hermeneutic Project, spring 1982 (unpublished).

10. Elisabeth Schüssler Fiorenza, "A Feminist Biblical Hermeneutics: Biblical Interpretation and Liberation Theology," in *The Challenge of Libera-*

tion Theology: A First-World Response, L. Dale Richesin and Brian Mahan, eds. (Orbis Books, 1981), p. 106.

11. Ruether, *Sexism and God Talk,* pp. 18–19.

12. Fiorenza, "A Feminist Biblical Hermeneutics," p. 108.

13. Fiorenza, "Response to the Responders," prepared for discussion at the AAR Meeting, December 1982, and circulated to the Liberation Theology Working Group (unpublished).

14. Fiorenza, "A Feminist Biblical Hermeneutics," p. 100.

15. Ibid., p. 107. In this volume, "patriarchy" refers not only to ancient societies where fathers ruled over women, children, and slaves but also to the prevailing systems of social, economic, and political oppression [127, 143].

16. Birch, "Response . . . ."

17. T. Drorah Setel, "A Jewish Feminist Response . . . ," Feminist Hermeneutic Project, spring 1982 (unpublished).

18. Vincent L. Wimbush, " 'Rescue the Perishing': The Importance of Biblical Scholarship in Black Christianity," *Reflection* 8(2):10 (January 1983).

1: Feminist Consciousness in Historical Perspective

1. *The Woman's Bible,* p. 11.

2. Bass, *JSOT* 22:6–12.

3. "An Essay on Slavery and Abolitionism with Reference to the Duty of Females," reprinted in Rosemary Radford Ruether and Rosemary Skinner Keller, eds., *Women and Religion in America,* vol. 1 (Harper & Row, 1981), p. 311.

4. Virginia Woolf, *Three Guineas* (Harcourt, Brace and Co., 1938, 1963), pp. 62–63 of 1963 edition.

5. Daly, *Beyond God the Father,* pp. 11–12.

2: The Emergence of Black Feminist Consciousness

1. C. Eric Lincoln, in his foreword to William R. Jones's *Is God a White Racist?* (Doubleday & Co., Anchor Books, 1973), pp. vii–viii.

2. Howard Thurman, *Deep River and the Negro Spiritual Speaks of Life and Death* (Friends United Press, 1975), p. 135.

3. Benjamin Mays, *The Negro's God as Reflected in His Literature* (Chapman & Grimes, 1938; reprint ed., Greenwood Press, 1969), p. 26.

4. George P. Rawick, *The American Slave: A Composite Autobiography, From Sundown to Sunup* (Greenwood Press, 1972), p. 51.

5. La Frances Rodgers-Rose, ed., *The Black Woman* (Sage Publications, 1980), p. 20.

6. Barbara Christian, *Black Women Novelists: The Development of a Tradition, 1892–1976* (Greenwood Press, 1980), p. 13.

7. Paul A. David et al., *Reckoning with Slavery: Critical Essays in the Quantitative History of American Negro Slavery* (Oxford University Press, 1976), p. 59. For a detailed discussion of the internal slave trade, see Frederic Bancroft, *Slave Trading in the Old South* (Frederick Ungar Publishing Co., 1959).

8. A quotation by Fannie Barrier Williams in *Black Women in Nineteenth-Century American Life: Their Words, Their Thoughts, Their Feelings*, ed. by Bert James Loewenberg and Ruth Bogin (Pennsylvania State University Press, 1976), p. 15.

9. Henry Allen Bullock, *A History of Negro Education in the South from 1619 to the Present* (Harvard University Press, 1967), pp. 155–156.

10. Stated by then Chief Justice Taney in the Dred Scott case, March 1857.

11. Jeanne L. Noble, *Beautiful, Also, Are the Souls of My Black Sisters: A History of the Black Woman in America* (Prentice-Hall, 1978), p. 63.

12. William J. Wilson, *Power, Racism, and Privilege: Race Relations in Theoretical and Sociohistorical Perspectives* (Macmillan Publishing Co., 1973), p. 99.

13. Pierre L. van den Berghe, *Race and Racism: A Comparative Perspective* (John Wiley & Sons, 1967), p. 77.

14. According to *Negro Population in the United States 1790–1915*, five Black women migrated out of the South for every four Black men.

15. Sharon Harley and Rosalyn Terborg-Penn, eds., *The Afro-American Woman, Struggles and Images* (Kennikat Press, 1978), p. 8.

16. Zora Neale Hurston, *Their Eyes Were Watching God* (J. B. Lippincott Co., 1937; reprint ed., University of Illinois Press, 1978), p. 34.

17. Alice Walker, *In Search of Our Mothers' Gardens: Womanist Prose* (Harcourt Brace Jovanovich, 1983), pp. xi–xii. Walker indicates that the term "Womanist" is "from womanish (opposite of 'girlish,' i.e., frivolous, 'irresponsible, not serious'). A black feminist or feminist of color." Among other things she loves women, is committed to the survival of her people and their culture, loves herself. "Womanist is to feminist as purple is to lavender."

3: Feminist Consciousness and the Interpretation of Scripture

1. See Paul Ricoeur, *Essays on Biblical Interpretation,* ed. by Lewis S. Mudge (Fortress Press, 1980), p. 95.

2. Ibid., pp. 49–72.

3. See, for example, Beverly Wildung Harrison, *Our Right to Choose: Toward a New Ethic of Abortion* (Beacon Press, 1983), chapter 3; James M. Gustafson, *The Contributions of Theology to Medical Ethics* (Marquette University Press, 1975), pp. 84–90; Richard A. McCormick, *How Brave a New World: Dilemmas in Bioethics* (Doubleday & Co., 1981), p. 9; Thomas W. Ogletree, *The Use of the Bible in Christian Ethics* (Fortress Press, 1983).

4: Feminist Uses of Biblical Materials

1. See David H. Kelsey, "The Bible and Christian Theology," *Journal of the American Academy of Religion* 48:400–401 (1980). Kelsey argues that scripture itself, even carefully read and rigorously studied, cannot ultimately adjudicate disputes over the basic character of Christianity. A certain commonality of perspective ("imaginative construal") is required, Kelsey suggests, before the Bible can function normatively in resolving faith differences or in approaching contemporary issues.

2. Letty Russell, *Growth in Partnership,* esp. pp. 88–103. The quotation is from p. 98.

3. Ruether, *Sexism and God Talk,* p. 23.

4. Ibid., p. 34.

5. Fiorenza, *In Memory of Her,* pp. 14–20.

6. Letty Russell's recent study guide for Ephesians develops the use of this option for group study. See *Imitators of God: A Study Book on Ephesians.*

7. Trible, *Texts of Terror,* p. 3.

8. Fiorenza, *In Memory of Her,* p. 92 [131].

5: A Gentile Woman's Story

1. Trible, "Feminist Hermeneutics and Biblical Studies"; Fiorenza, *In Memory of Her.*

2. Luke does not tell the woman's story at all. If he knew the story from Mark's Gospel, he apparently chose not to repeat it. In fact, Luke's Gospel does not contain a series of accounts clustered at this point in Mark (Mark 6:45—7:26), all of which deal with Jesus' relationship to Gentiles. Thus it may be that the omission of this story was part of a broader decision.

3. In Matthew the woman speaks of dogs receiving crumbs from "the master's table," whereas in Mark she responds in a way more directly

parallel to Jesus' words to her (JESUS: Children's bread not thrown to dogs; WOMAN: Dogs under the table eat the children's crumbs [Ringe]). The saying in verse 27 of Mark ("Let the children first be fed") appears to be an editorial addition to the story, since there is no suggestion in the narrative that the woman has forced herself onto Jesus' agenda ahead of anyone else. Note also similar sayings in Romans 1:6 and 2:10.

4. That coherence is evident despite some variation in wording in the account. The cause of the daughter's distress is called an "unclean spirit" in verse 25 but a "demon" elsewhere. It must be noted that the different word occurs only in the setting, which was probably supplied by Mark. That same introductory verse also contains the only instance where the daughter is called by the diminutive word "little daughter"; elsewhere she is called "daughter," except in the concluding verse, where she is called a "child." That last term echoes the one used in the woman's reply to Jesus in verse 28. In a sense, then, the variations interweave even more tightly the components of the story.

5. Rudolf Bultmann, *The History of the Synoptic Tradition* (Harper & Row, 1963), p. 38. This view is held by many scholars, including Eduard Schweizer, *The Good News According to Mark* (John Knox Press, 1970), p. 151; Vincent Taylor, *The Gospel According to St. Mark* (Macmillan Co., 1957), p. 347; Willi Marxsen, *Mark the Evangelist* (Abingdon Press, 1969), p. 60.

6. Taylor, *The Gospel According to St. Mark*, p. 350.

7. Howard Clark Kee, *Community of the New Age* (Westminster Press, 1977), p. 83.

8. The conclusion that the issue of Jewish-Gentile relations represents a later interpretation of the story is further supported by details in Matthew's version. First, there the woman is identified not by the political or geographic designation of "Greek" or "Syrophoenician" but rather as a "Canaanite," the term common in Hebrew scriptures to refer to those most clearly not part of the chosen people. Second, Jesus' initial response to the woman's request sets her apart from the "lost sheep of the house of Israel" to whom he has been sent. Finally, Matthew breaks the homely metaphor of the Markan account, so that the "dogs" no longer simply get to eat up the crumbs that the children drop but rather are entitled to the leftovers from the master's table.

9. T. A. Burkill, "The Story of the Syrophoenician Woman," *Novum Testamentum* 9:173 (1967).

10. J.D.M. Derett ("Law in the New Testament: The Syrophoenician Woman and the Centurion of Capernaum," *Novum Testamentum* 15:162 [1973]) points out that this is a common resolution by both the church and the scholarly community to the unacceptable portrait of Jesus that is presented here.

11. Taylor, *The Gospel According to St. Mark*, p. 350.

12. See the discussion of laws and customs affecting women in first-century Palestine in Chapter XVIII ("Appendix: The Social Position of Women") of Joachim Jeremias, *Jerusalem in the Time of Jesus* (Fortress Press, 1969), pp. 359–376.

6: "Mother in Israel": A Familiar Figure Reconsidered

1. Research for this study was conducted with the support of a grant from the Penrose Fund of the American Philosophical Society.

2. Translation of the Song of Deborah is difficult and debated. Here I follow the RSV; for different views see, e.g., David Noel Freedman, *Pottery, Poetry and Prophecy: Studies in Early Hebrew Poetry* (Eisenbrauns, 1980), p. 150; J. Alberto Soggin, *Judges* (Westminster Press, 1981), pp. 81–82, 85–86.

3. Besides the works listed in Additional Resources, see Samuel Terrien, "Toward a Biblical Theology of Womanhood," *Religion in Life* 42:322–333 (1973); reprinted in Ruth T. Barnhouse and Urban T. Holmes, eds., *Male and Female: Christian Approaches to Sexuality* (Seabury Press, 1976), pp. 17–27; Frederick E. Greenspahn, "A Typology of Biblical Women," *Judaism* 32: 43–50 (1983). For a provocative statement on "Reading as a Woman" influenced by the work of feminist literary critics, see Jonathan Culler, *On Deconstruction: Theory and Criticism After Structuralism* (Routledge & Kegan Paul, 1982), pp. 43–64.

4. See, for example, Carol Meyers, "Procreation, Production, and Protection: Male–Female Balance in Early Israel," *Journal of the American Academy of Religion* 51:569–593 (1983).

5. See pp. 42–66 of *Women Recounted: Narrative Thinking and the God of Israel* (Sheffield: Almond Press, 1982), by James G. Williams, who treats, in addition to those discussed here, Zipporah, Hannah, and the woman of Shunem (1 Kings 4).

6. On Eve, see especially Trible, *God and the Rhetoric of Sexuality*, pp. 72–143.

7. On point of view, see Adele Berlin's *Poetics and Interpretation of Biblical Narrative* (Sheffield: Almond Press, 1983), for a discussion of a number of biblical women.

8. John Van Seters's *Abraham in History and Tradition* (Yale University Press, 1975), p. 193, puts it nicely: "The son to be born to her will have a destiny that will be anything but submissive and his defiance will be her ultimate vindication." Notice again, however, that the mother's importance derives from her son.

9. Following M. Cogan, "A Technical Term for Exposure" (*Journal of Near Eastern Studies* 27:133–135 [1968]), in taking the verb to mean "abandon, expose" (RSV, "cast into").

10. B. S. Childs, "The Birth of Moses," *Journal of Biblical Literature* 84: 112–114 (1965).

11. J. Cheryl Exum, " 'You Shall Let Every Daughter Live': A Study of Exodus 1:8—2:10," in Tolbert, pp. 63–82.

12. I have demonstrated how the literary structure of Judges 13 supports the emphasis on the woman in "Promise and Fulfillment: Narrative Art in Judges 13," *Journal of Biblical Literature* 99:43–59 (1980). For a different evaluation of the woman, see Robert Polzin, *Moses and the Deuteronomist: A Literary Study of the Deuteronomic History* (Seabury Press, 1980), pp. 181–184.

13. See the amended text of 1 Samuel 12:11; also Hebrews 11:32.

14. P. C. Craigie, "Deborah and Anat: A Study of Poetic Imagery," *Zeitschrift für die alttestamentliche Wissenschaft* 90:374–381 (1978).

15. For a detailed, insightful treatment of the portrayal of the women in Judges 4 vis-à-vis the men, see D. F. Murray, "Narrative Structure and Technique in the Deborah–Barak Story (Judges IV 4-22)," *Vetus Testamentum Supplements* 30:166–183 (1979).

16. Judges 5:1 had Deborah and Barak as the subject, but the verb is third person feminine singular. Debates about whether or not she really composed or sang the song are useless exercises in historical literalism.

17. Craigie, pp. 377–378, takes the title as a reference to Deborah's emergence as a military leader.

18. The only other appearance of the title "mother in Israel" is in reference to a city, 2 Samuel 20:19, where it appears to have the same range of meanings. On the mother and "mother in Israel," see also Claudia U. Camp, "The Wise Women of 2 Samuel: A Role Model for Women in Early Israel?" *Catholic Biblical Quarterly* 43:24–28 (1981).

7: Prophets and Pornography: Female Sexual Imagery in Hosea

1. I believe it cannot be emphasized strongly enough that the Hebrew Bible and the culture from which it emerged do *not* represent the origins of patriarchy. For further discussion of this issue and its implications, see Judith Plaskow, "Blaming the Jews for the Birth of Patriarchy," in Evelyn T. Beck, ed., *Nice Jewish Girls: A Lesbian Anthology* (Persephone Press, 1982), pp. 250–254.

I would alike to acknowledge and thank the women of Benot Esh for the community in which I was able to ask the questions which led to this article.

2. Simone de Beauvoir, *The Second Sex* (Penguin Books, 1976), pp. 11–29.

3. The following outline draws on Andrea Dworkin, *Our Blood* and *Pornography;* Susan Griffin, *Woman and Nature* (Harper & Row, 1978); Laura Led-

erer, ed., *Take Back the Night* (William Morrow & Co., 1980); and Robin Morgan, ed., *Going Too Far* (Vintage Books, 1978).

4. Dworkin, *Our Blood*, p. 110.

5. Irene Diamond, "Pornography and Repression: A Reconsideration of 'Who' and 'What,' " in Lederer, pp. 187–203.

6. Dworkin, *Pornography*, p. 18.

7. Ibid., pp. 199–202.

8. Adrienne Rich, "Afterword," in Lederer, pp. 313–320.

9. Helen E. Longino, "Pornograph, Oppression, and Freedom: A Closer Look," in Lederer, pp. 40–54.

10. Dworkin, *Pornography*, pp. 199–202.

11. Ibid., pp. 13–47, 199–202.

12. Diamond, in Lederer, p. 192.

13. Carol Meyers, "The Roots of Restriction," *Biblical Archaeologist* (Sept. 1978), pp. 91–103; Carol Meyers, "Procreation, Production, and Protection: Male–Female Balance in Early Israel," *Journal of the American Academy of Religion* 51:569–593 (1983).

14. For clarity I have used the modern (rather than linguistic) method of transliteration, given in Werner Weinberg, ed., *Guide to Hebrew Transliteration* (Union of American Hebrew Congregations, 1974).

15. I would like to acknowledge and thank Mr. Hyam Maccoby of the Leo Baeck College, London, for this and other insights related to the *tum'ah/taharah* system.

16. The significance of the ongoing aspect of this priestly reattribution of power to the deity is discussed in Nancy Jay, "Throughout Your Generations Forever: A Sociology of Blood Sacrifice" (unpublished dissertation, Department of Sociology, Brandeis University, 1981).

17. I would like to thank Jo Ann Hackett of Cambridge, Massachusetts, for sharing the discussions which led to some of these insights. For a summary of the textual bases of female status, see Phyllis Trible, "Woman in the OT," *The Interpreter's Dictionary of the Bible*, Supplementary Volume (Abingdon Press, 1976), pp. 963–966.

18. Norman Gottwald, *The Tribes of Yahweh* (Orbis Books, 1979), pp. 557–558.

19. Biblical quotations are adapted from Herbert G. May and Bruce M. Metzger, eds., *The New Oxford Annotated Bible* (Revised Standard Version) (Oxford University Press, 1977). Chapter and verse references are according to the divisions of the Masoretic Text of the Hebrew Bible.

20. Francis I. Andersen and David Noel Freedman, trans., *Hosea* (Doubleday & Co., 1980), p. 157.

21. Ibid., pp. 157–158.

22. Ibid., p. 43.

8: Every Two Minutes: Battered Women and Feminist Interpretation

1. *Crisis: Women's Experience and the Church's Response. Final Report of a Crisis Survey of United Methodists,* The United Methodist Church (March 1982), pp. 4–9.

2. Ibid.

3. R. Emerson Dobash and Russell Dobash, *Violence Against Wives* (Free Press, 1979), pp. 33–34. Italics added.

4. John B. Cobb, Jr., *Process Theology as Political Theology* (Westminster Press, 1982), p. 23.

5. Lenore E. Walker, *The Battered Woman* (Harper & Row, 1979), p. 31.

6. Juan Luis Segundo, *The Liberation of Theology* (Orbis Books, 1976), p. 9.

7. Justo L. Gonzalez and Catherine G. Gonzalez, *Liberation Preaching.*

8. Raymond E. Brown, "Roles of Women in the Fourth Gospel," *Theological Studies* 36:688–689 (1975), reprinted in *Community of the Beloved Disciple* (Paulist Press, 1979), pp. 183–198.

9. Rudolf Schnackenburg, *The Gospel According to St. John* (Seabury Press, 1980), p. 165.

10. Fleming, *Stopping,* pp. 73–74, quoted from *Introduction to Battered Women: One Testimony* (Southwest Community Mental Health Center, Columbus, Ohio). Italics added.

11. "Declaration on the Question of Admission of Women to the Priesthood," in Leonard and Arlene Swidler, eds., *Women Priests: Catholic Commentary on the Vatican Declaration* (Paulist Press, 1977).

12. Elisabeth Schüssler Fiorenza, "The Twelve," in Swidler and Swidler, *Women Priests,* p. 138.

13. Lenore Walker has identified a three-stage cycle to the violence in homes of batterers: the "tension-building stage," the "acute battering incident," the "kindness and contrite, loving behavior" stage. Walker notes that women who kill their abusers do so in stage three. *The Battered Woman,* pp. 55–70.

14. Dobash and Dobash, *Violence Against Wives,* p. 205.

15. Trible, *God and the Rhetoric . . .* , pp. 95–102.

16. Walter Brueggemann, "Of the Same Flesh and Bone, Genesis 2:23a," *Catholic Biblical Quarterly* 32:532 (1969).

17. Ibid., p. 541.

18. Adrienne Rich, "Natural Resources," in her *The Dream of a Common Language: Poems 1974–1977* (W. W. Norton & Co., 1978), p. 185.

10: The Will to Choose or to Reject: Continuing Our Critical Work

1. Adrienne Rich, "Vesuvius at Home: The Power of Emily Dickinson (1975)," in *On Lies, Secrets, and Silence, Selected Prose 1966–1978* (W. W. Norton & Co., 1979), p. 172.

2. Carol P. Christ, "Why Women Need the Goddess: Phenomenological, Psychological, and Political Reflections," in Carol P. Christ and Judith Plaskow, eds., *Womanspirit Rising: A Feminist Reader in Religion* (Harper & Row, 1979), pp. 273–287.

3. Alice Bloch, "Scenes from the Life of a Jewish Lesbian," in Susannah Heschel, ed., *On Being a Jewish Feminist: A Reader* (Schocken Books, 1983), p. 174.

4. In speaking about a feminist biblical interpretation, I also do not want to imply that feminist Jewish and Christian biblical interpretations are the same or must develop along the same lines. As Drorah Setel has rightly pointed out, references to the "Judeo-Christian" tradition or heritage ignore the significant inequalities in that relationship. However, insofar as the Old Testament or Hebrew Bible is part of the Christian Bible, a feminist Christian hermeneutics must deal with the Jewish Bible while a Jewish feminist hermeneutics does not need to pay attention to the New Testament.

5. For definition and discussion of patriarchy, see, for example, Heidi Hartmann, "Capitalism, Patriarchy, and Job Segregation by Sex," in Elizabeth and Emily K. Abel, eds., *The Signs Reader: Women, Gender, and the Scholarship* (University of Chicago Press, 1983), pp. 193–225.

6. "Redstockings: April 1969"; reprinted in *Feminist Revolution* (Random House, 1975), p. 205.

7. See my "Toward a Feminist Biblical Hermeneutics," in *The Challenge of Liberation Theology*, pp. 91–112, which was presented in 1979 at a conference sponsored by Chicago Divinity School.

8. Adrienne Rich, "Disloyal to Civilization: Feminism, Fascism, Gynephobia (1978)," in *On Lies . . .* , p. 307.

9. Ntozake Shange's ending chorus is often quoted by religious feminists. However, it must not be overlooked that such an affirmation is only

achieved in and through the experience and naming of racist-sexist patriarchal oppressions. *For Colored Girls Who Have Considered Suicide/When the Rainbow Is Enuf: A Choreopoem* (Macmillan Publishing Co., 1977).

10. Marcia Westkott, "Women's Studies as a Strategy for Change: Between Criticism and Vision," in Gloria Bowles and Renate Duelli-Klein, eds., *Theories of Women's Studies* (Routledge & Kegan Paul, 1983), p. 213.

11. For example, Shirley Rogers Radl, *The Invisible Woman: Target of the Religious New Right* (Delta Books, 1983).

12. Betty Willis Brooks and Sharon L. Sievers, "The New Right Challenges Women's Studies: The Long Beach Women's Studies Program," in Charlotte Bunch and Sandra Pollack, eds., *Learning Our Way: Essays in Feminist Education* (Crossing Press, 1983), pp. 78–88.

13. *We Continue Forever: Sorrow and Strength of Guatemalan Women* (International Resource Exchange, 1983), p. 18.

14. See my collection of essays on feminist biblical interpretation *Bread Not Stone: Introduction to a Feminist Interpretation of Scripture* (Beacon Press, 1985).

15. See the overview and discussion of David Tracy, "Particular Questions Within General Consensus," in Leonard Swidler, ed., *Consensus in Theology?* (Westminster Press, 1980), pp. 33–39.

16. See John P. Clayton, "Was ist falsch in der Korrelationstheorie?", *Neue Zeitschrift für Systematische Theologie* 16:93–111 (1974), and Francis Schüssler Fiorenza, *Foundational Theology: Jesus and the Church* (Crossroad, 1984), to whom I am indebted for this reference.

17. Charlene Spretnack, "The Christian Right's 'Holy War' Against Feminism," in *The Politics of Women's Spirituality* (Doubleday & Co., Anchor Books, 1982), pp. 470–496.

11: Authority and the Challenge of Feminist Interpretation

1. Fiorenza, *In Memory of Her*, p. 34.

2. See "Theology as Anticipation" in my *Growth in Partnership*, pp. 87–109.

3. Tolbert, "Defining the Problem," in *The Bible and Feminist Hermeneutics*, p. 120.

4. Sallie McFague, *Metaphorical Theology* (Fortress Press, 1982), pp. 79–83.

5. Vincent L. Wimbush, " 'Rescue the Perishing': The Importance of Biblical Scholarship in Black Christianity," *Reflection*, 8(2):10 (January 1983).

6. See Phyllis Bird's discussion of how scripture is understood as Word of God in *The Bible as the Church's Book* (Westminster Press, 1982).

7. David H. Kelsey, *The Uses of Scripture in Recent Theology* (Fortress Press, 1975), p. 194. See also pages 167–175.

8. Ibid., p. 175.

9. McFague is building on the work of Thomas S. Kuhn, *The Structure of Scientific Revolutions,* 2nd ed., enlarged (University of Chicago Press, 1970), p. 175.

10. From a panel presentation on Feminist Hermeneutics, American Academy of Religion, San Francisco, December 20, 1983 (unpublished).

11. See also Phyllis Trible, *Texts of Terror.*

12. McFague, *Metaphorical Theology,* p. 82.

13. The problem of the paradigm of domination is discussed in L. Russell, "Women and Ministry: Problem or Possibility," *Christian Feminism,* Judith L. Weidman, ed. (Harper & Row, 1984), pp. 75–92.

14. Fiorenza, "Feminist Biblical Interpretation," *Christian Feminism,* p. 34.

15. Birch, "Response to Elisabeth Schüssler Fiorenza," panel presentation on feminist hermeneutics, American Academy of Religion, New York, December 20, 1982 (unpublished).

Postscript: Jottings on the Journey

1. The principle of liberation holds regardless of one's assessment of allegorical exegesis. Ample evidence can be found in Robert M. Grant with David Tracy, *A Short History of the Interpretation of the Bible* (Fortress Press, 1984), and Beryl Smallery, *The Study of the Bible in the Middle Ages* (University of Notre Dame Press, 1978).

2. For example, J. Severino Croatto, *Exodus: A Hermeneutics of Freedom* (Orbis Books, 1981).

3. Yet the feminist critique of scripture also has a history; see chapter 1 by Barbara Brown Zikmund.

4. For a fuller explanation, see B. W. Anderson, "God, Names of," *The Interpreter's Dictionary of the Bible,* vol. 2 (Abingdon Press, 1962), pp. 409, 414.

5. These comments do not intend approval either for *An Inclusive-Language Lectionary,* recently published by the National Council of Churches (1983, 1984) or for many of the criticisms leveled against it. More excellent ways await discovery.

6. For the traditional formulation, see, e.g., G. Ernest Wright, *The Old Testament and Theology* (Harper & Row, 1969), pp. 166–185. For criticisms,

see Brevard S. Childs, *Biblical Theology in Crisis* (Westminster Press, 1970) and *Introduction to the Old Testament as Scripture* (Fortress Press, 1979).

7. See James A. Sanders, *Canon and Community* (Fortress Press, 1984), pp. 21–60.

8. On sociological analysis, the work of Carol L. Meyers merits attention: "The Roots of Restriction: Women in Early Israel," in *The Bible and Liberation,* Norman K. Gottwald, ed. (Orbis Books, 1983), pp. 289–306; "Procreation, Production, and Protection: Male–Female Balance in Early Israel," *Journal of the American Academy of Religion* 51:569–593 (1983); "Gender Roles and Genesis 3:16 Revisited," in *The Word of the Lord Shall Go Forth,* Carol L. Meyers and M. O'Connor, eds. (Eisenbrauns, 1984), pp. 337–354.

Additional Resources

An Inclusive Language Lectionary: Readings for Year A. National Council of the Churches of Christ in the U.S.A. John Knox Press, Pilgrim Press, Westminster Press, 1983. *Readings for Year B,* 1984.

Bell, Roseann P., Bettye Parker, and Beverly Shetall, eds. *Sturdy Black Bridges: Visions of Black Women in Literature.* Doubleday & Co., 1978.

Bird, Phyllis A. *The Bible as the Church's Book.* Westminster Press, 1982.

Christ, Carol P., and Judith Plaskow. *Womanspirit Rising: A Feminist Reader in Religion.* Harper & Row, 1979.

Crotwell, Helen. *Women and the Word: Sermons.* Fortress Press, 1977.

Daly, Mary. *Beyond God the Father: Toward a Philosophy of Women's Liberation.* Beacon Press, 1973.

Dworkin, Andrea. *Our Blood.* Perigee, 1976.

———. *Pornography.* Perigee, 1981.

Fiorenza, Elisabeth Schüssler. *In Memory of Her: A Feminist Theological Reconstruction of Christian Origins.* Crossroad, 1983.

Giddings, Paula. *When and Where I Enter: The Impact of Black Women on Race and Sex in America.* William Morrow & Co., 1984.

Gonzalez, Justo L., and Catherine G. Gonzalez. *Liberation Preaching: The Pulpit and the Oppressed.* Abingdon Press, 1980.

Lindsay, Beverly, ed. *Comparative Perspectives of Third World Women: The Impact of Race, Sex, and Class.* Praeger Publishers, 1980.

McFague, Sallie. *Metaphorical Theology: Models of God in Religious Language.* Fortress Press, 1982.

Maguire, Daniel. "The Feminization of God and Ethics," *Christianity and Crisis* 42(4):63–66 (March 15, 1982).

Mahan, Brian, and L. Dale Richesin, eds. *The Challenge of Liberation Theology: A First World Response.* Orbis Books, 1981.

Mollenkott, Virginia Ramey. *Women, Men, and the Bible.* Abingdon Press, 1977.

Moraga, Cherrie, and Gloria Anzaldua, eds. *This Bridge Called My Back: Writings by Radical Women of Color.* Persephone Press, 1981.

Richardson, Marilyn. *Black Women and Religion: A Bibliography.* G. K. Hall & Co., 1980.

Ringe, Sharon. *Jesus and the Jubilee: Images in Ethics and Christology.* Fortress Press, 1985.

Ruether, Rosemary Radford, ed. *Religion and Sexism.* Simon & Schuster, 1974.

———. *Sexism and God Talk: Toward a Feminist Theology.* Beacon Press, 1983.

——— and Eleanor McLaughlin. *Women of Spirit.* Simon & Schuster, 1979.

Russell, Letty M. *Growth in Partnership.* Westminster Press, 1981.

———. *Imitators of God: A Study Book on Ephesians.* General Board of Global Ministries, United Methodist Church, 1984.

———, ed. *The Liberating Word: A Guide to Nonsexist Interpretation of the Bible.* Westminster Press, 1976.

Sakenfeld, Kathrine Doob. *Faithfulness in Action: Loyalty in Biblical Perspective.* Fortress Press, 1985.

Schaef, Ann Wilson. *Women's Reality: An Emerging Female System in the White Male Society.* Winston Press, 1981.

Stanton, Elizabeth Cady, and the Revising Committee. *The Woman's Bible.* European Publishing Co., 1898.

Tolbert, Mary Ann, ed. *The Bible and Feminist Hermeneutics* (Semeia 28). Scholars Press, 1983.

Trible, Phyllis. *God and the Rhetoric of Sexuality.* Fortress Press, 1978.

———. *Texts of Terror.* Fortress Press, 1984.

Whalberg, Rachel Conrad. *Jesus According to a Woman.* Paulist Press, 1975.

———. *Jesus and the Freed Woman.* Paulist Press, 1978.